Eight
Was Enough

A God-Led Adventure with
Adopted & Special Needs Kids

By

Trisha K. Campbell

PRO
ZOE
PUBLISHING

prozoepublishing@gmail.com

ISBN: 978-1-7374847-0-7 (print)
ISBN: 978-1-7374847-1-4 (ebook)

Ordering Information:
Special discounts are available on quantity purchases by corporations, associations, and others. For details, contact prozoepublishing@gmail.com.

TABLE OF CONTENTS

Preface

Our current culture asserts that the adoption of Black children into White families is an expression of "White Supremacy." Accusations have been leveled that "White colonizers" take Black children from their heritage. If you have this opinion and want to hold onto it, you better stop reading. If you wonder if it's true or not, read on.

An extraordinarily disproportionate number of aborted children are Black—over 500,000 annually during the time we were adopting. Proponents of abortion scream for pro-life people to step up and care for the kids that are born. We did. We accepted a divine calling for a heavenly purpose and responded in loving obedience to the call. It was a long, hard, and often painful road. It still is. And I'd do it all over again if given the choice. Parenting is the hardest job I've ever loved.

Life's an adventure or nothing at all.

—*Helen Keller*

You never begin the Christian journey until you hear
God's voice. It is heard when the Word of God is brought home
to our hearts by the Spirit of God.

—*Alistair Begg, my pastor for the last 20 years*

Prologue
The Voice

A bruptly awakened from a sound sleep, I heard a clear voice say, "Jobe." The name sounded vaguely familiar, but I couldn't place it. As my eyes acclimated to the darkness, my ears registered my husband's gentle snore. I *heard* the still voice inside me, which was somewhat new to me. I recall thinking it was strange, but a number of women in my current Bible study often said things like "God told me this" or "God showed me that," so I thought perhaps this was a similar situation where my physical ears weren't involved. I wrote J-O-B-E on a notepad kept by my bed.

Then, I lazily *rolled over and went back to sleep.*

The God of the universe may have spoken to me, and I rolled over and went back to sleep?!

Even though I recognized it as scripture, I didn't search for it, not even the next day. It was as if the queen of England had called me to teatime or Albert Einstein wanted to give me a science lesson, and I just didn't heed their invitations! I guess I didn't have the genuine conviction I was actually hearing from God. My nonchalant attitude blows my mind in retrospect.

Then, it happened *again*.

This time, it wasn't the inner voice; rather, I woke with a full line of text running incessantly through my head. "In Him, there is no darkness at all … in Him, there is no darkness at all," over and over. *Who* isn't dark? What's going on? Lying awake, blinking in the predawn blackness, I could *not* go back to sleep because the word loop just didn't stop. I hauled my still tired, sleepy body out of bed and made it join my now wired, awake brain. I padded downstairs, noticing the rare sound of silence in my young family home that had three small children.

But my spirit within was anything *but* quiet.

Going to the dining room, I knelt on the carpeted floor and asked God about this incessant repetitive line that had been running on a nonstop treadmill in my brain. As I knelt with my head down on the carpet, my hands clasped in prayer, a poem started to form in my mind's eye.

Fearful it might just slip away, I went to my desk, grabbed one of my ubiquitous notepads, and began to write. Via one long, continuous flow, a three-stanza poem just came forth from the pen like a river of life in ink:

> Original Sin began at the Fall,
> Our nature determined, for each one and all.
> Cut off from our God, some way to begin,
> Our spirits cut off by Original Sin.

The Lord sent His Son, such mercy has He.
He came as the Savior, for you and for me.
Now Jesus has come, we all can stand tall,
In Him there is no darkness at all.

Reunion with God, we can now complete.
The Sinner's Prayer, we all must repeat.
Ask Christ in your life, He will come in,
Corrected you now, the Original Sin.

That line again—right in the middle! "In Him, there is no darkness at all!"

But I didn't know what to *do* with it.

Then, I remembered the inner voice from the other night and my negligence in following through on its origin. I thought to myself to read the book of Jobe, which had awakened me a couple of nights ago. Requiring a bit of time, since I was new to Bible study, I struggled to find the book and was dumbfounded when I did—it was spelled like the word "job"! As I read Job's difficult story, I discovered that God had been reading *me* like a book—He knew me and *my* story.

"I read books to understand them. What is this book (holding up his Bible) that actually understands me?"

–Alistair Begg

1

The Odyssey

My story is not for the faint of heart. Life started in New England where I came from salt-of-the-earth stock. My irrepressible father, a regional Boston police officer, and my sensible mother, a teacher turned stay-at-home mom, believed you could do anything if you applied ample thought, good old hard work, and Yankee ingenuity! When I was four, we moved into a long-neglected towering turreted Queen Ann Victorian—my father quipped it only had two fixer-upper jobs, the inside and the outside. Five years in, Dad had barely gotten the house project livable when he had a wonderful idea—our family should build a summer cabin *from scratch* in the remote woods of Maine.

Leaving no room for dissension, Dad told us little of his plans until he was ready to execute the project. We arrived in the second week of July for our camping "vacation" on our 70 acres of woods in Dresden Mills, Maine. My father arranged the deep woods trip at the time the *Farmers' Almanac* said the "sap was running." On the first day, we were told that

The towering turreted Queen Anne Victorian Melrose House.

over the next two weeks we were going to cut down and skin a hundred trees to build a cabin, just like our Lincoln logs toy set at home.

Dad, with the chainsaw, and the rest of us, armed with old *butter knives,* went through the woods every day, taking down trees one at a time; Dad took down the trees and removed all the branches with the saw, then we scored the bark with our butter knives and peeled it off. We were half-choked by the fumes of the saw, but the flying wood chips that flew in our eyes and settled to stick on our pine-pitched skin were far more irritating. Often, halfway through the day, Dad's sweat-sodden shirt would come off and wood chips knit their way into his red arm and chest hair, adding dimension to his pale, freckled Irish complexion. Our mom was up ahead of us where she marked the next good and straight pine for my dad and happily stayed ahead of the pine-tar pitch and wood confetti.

Each workday ended with a clean-up swim in the icy cold waters of the "Minnissippi." It was a name we gave the melted snow stream running through our property. Though not near the stream or the campfire, gasoline was used to remove sticky sap from our hands and forearms. It was my dad's dubious choice of solvents. During those long, arduous workweeks, no one had any difficulty sleeping at night! We wore the same lousy clothes every day because they were soaked with sap, which stiffened overnight as we slept like logs in our tents. Each morning, we walked about to loosen the hardened sappy fabric of our jeans.

And for our trouble? To keep us motivated, dad promised to give each of us 10 whole dollars when we finished. Ten! As a nine-year-old, I rarely saw such largess, as the typical birthday card from a relative had a dollar, maybe two. We laid on the lumpy tent floor in our sleeping bags as we dreamed of the many wonderful things 10 dollars could buy. I'd done the math, and that was 100 dime-store comic books!

After the initial lumberjack vacation, we had to let the logs dry for a year. Then, we spent the next couple of summers building the cabin and adding "niceties" to make life easier. For instance, we added a rain barrel. This wonderful accessory meant we no longer had to schlep buckets of water the 10-minute walk over the rutted old loggers' road from the Minnissippi with deer flies buzzing in our ears! It was a tragedy when you had to swat at nettlesome biting flies and then spill your buckets of liquid gold, necessitating a return trip to the stream. After the rainwater system was installed, dad would joke that we had "running water" because it ran down the roof into the rain barrel!

Then we put in gas lines for interior lighting. We would save the flashlight batteries for the midnight treks to the outhouse—down the path "a piece," away from the cabin, keeping its scented aura at a distance. We also built a big rough-hewn plank porch and a bunk room in case someone didn't want to climb into the rather crowded sleeping loft. All these add-ons made life in the Maine woods much easier, though most people likely consider them hardships.

Liz and I working the log lug and Peter in the background with a chain saw.

My parents did whatever they believed to be best for our family; teaching us right from wrong, economy, industry, faith in religion, value of education, love of family, beauty in nature—all the elements that should give a foundation to a good and perfect life. I arrived in young adulthood with my family's quirky yet firm foundation and tried so hard to do everything right, but I felt something was still wrong. Was something wrong with me or just in general?

According to the adults in my life at the time, satisfaction and joy were my rewards if I did things just the way they were supposed to be done. I desperately wanted to please my parents, teachers, coaches, and neighbors—but I couldn't do it. I tried so hard to be perfect, and my siblings teased me about my bedroom "looking like a museum." I often rearranged it and got rid of every bit of dust or clutter trying to make it a peaceful perfect place. At school, when my teacher assigned a two-page paper on a subject, I gave her five—just to be sure I covered all aspects of the subject. I tried to control the parts of my life I could control, but doing so fueled a tremulous undercurrent of anxiety. I thought if I found the truth about life and living, it would give me the elusive peace and contentment I sought.

"No man knows how bad he is until he has tried to be good."

—*C.S. Lewis*

The Keating Family: John, Dad (Paul), Mum (Helen), Liz, and Pete and I are in the back row.

I knew faith was supposed to help, but my religious Catholic education failed to communicate to me the full Good News of the Gospel, which was the part I really needed to obtain peace with God. In my early college years, I started to look for answers to life's toughest questions:

Where did I come from?

Where am I going?

How did I get here?

What am I doing here?

Why does it matter?

Who even cares?

"The truth must be in God," I thought. "He knows everything, but He is so unapproachable," or so I believed. I was taught to revere and fear Him, but as a Catholic, I was told I didn't have any direct access to Him. I was taught I could reach Him through priests and nuns. If I went to church, went to CCD class (Catholic doctrinal education for kids that go to public schools), said my prayers, went to confession, took my first Communion, made confirmation, and jumped through all the religious "hoops," then *they* would intercede *for* me.

But it did not work—I was willing and obedient to follow all the religiosity presented to me, yet I was still incapable of getting things right. I couldn't make my life perfect or even peaceful as the undercurrent of anxiety seemed to flow through every aspect of my existence. Then, I thought to check the Bible, but I was a bit apprehensive as I'd never been taught that I was *allowed* to read it. We were told only the priests had the authority to let us know what we needed to hear from the religious text. So, during my childhood, we literally dusted the Bible off when we cleaned the house but never really opened it.

So, I painstakingly wrote long letters to both my godparents with the details of my spiritual struggle, and I asked for their help. After all, they were *god*parents, right? This must be why I was given them! I waited patiently, checked my college mailbox daily with anxious anticipation, but received no answers from either one—not even an acknowledgment of my intellectual and spiritual struggles.

It frustrated me because, at the very least, I could have felt some kinship in my ignorance if they had acknowledged their lack of answers. But with no reply, I felt set adrift on my sea of challenging philosophical questions with no paddle of insight to direct me forward in a given direction. I didn't know where to turn or what to think, but I refused to allow the sea of questions to go unanswered or drown me. I don't know if it was sheer curiosity or dogged stubbornness, but I kept on.

As a college government major in the late 1970s and early '80s, I kept close track of the news and how it impacted my existential questions alongside my college studies. I had a wary eye on the violence in Central America during the Nicaraguan Revolution and the Salvadoran Civil War, often targeted at the Catholic Church. Priests and nuns were brutally raped and murdered by guerrilla insurgents, and even archbishops weren't protected. I was horrified to read that Óscar Arnulfo Romero y Galdámez was found in a pool of his own blood, gunned down in El Salvador in March of 1980. Catholicism didn't seem to be helping these missionary paragons of the church, so why would it hold any answers about peace and protection for me, a mere parishioner?

After I received no direction from my Catholic godparents, and with no clear insight or direction from my religion, I once again turned elsewhere. Instead of just looking beyond my religion, I decided to look beyond Christianity altogether.

So, I threw out the baby Jesus with the religious bathwater.

Over the next decade, I delved into and dabbled with Taoism (the teachings of Lao-Tze), Buddhism (the teachings of Buddha), Christian Science (the teachings of Mary Baker Eddy), New Age (astrology, reincarnation, spiritual energy, and the like), and even Scientology (man is basically good, and his salvation depends on himself). None of these explorations helped me figure out the source of my torment, nor did they show me how to be saved from my self-imposed prison of perfectionism.

Thankfully, I was looking for the truth, and this protected my spirit from being completely sucked into all those flawed theologies. I wasn't looking to feel better about myself, earn more, get further in life, or discover the secret of the cosmos. I wanted to know the *truth* about life and living and the answers to my questions about existence and its meaning. So, even though I didn't know this was biblical at the time, scriptural truth protected me from all the psychological, philosophical, and theological garbage I delved into:

"Ask, and it will be given to you; seek, and you will find; knock, and it will be opened to you."

(Matthew 7:7 English Standard Version)

I wanted honest answers, and God Himself was going to make sure I found them.

"And you will know the truth, and the truth will set you free."

(John 8:32)

The truth and power implicit in these scriptures were still at work on my behalf even though I didn't know they were in the Bible.

Truth is truth, whether you believe it or not.

My existentialist questions and research continued in parallel with my college education. My independent study for my government and politics major was Population and Food Problems in Developing Countries: A Foreign Policy Analysis. My studies lit a desire in me to go to a underdeveloped country and see conditions for myself. My advisor at Bowdoin College in Brunswick, Maine, came up with a plan for me to earn college credit and stay on track to graduate. I went to San Diego State University and became a teacher's assistant for an upper-level government class. Also, I took some additional classes and worked on a hunger project just over the border in Tijuana, Mexico.

We worked with the hunger outreach in Tijuana's Tecolote and Obrera dumps, and it was quite a scene; corrugated cardboard and metal fashioned into makeshift dwellings, dust-clogged air, emaciated cows foraged in the garbage, and lice-riddled, ragged children laughed and played in the filth.

It amazed me as I witnessed people cut off rotten portions of tortilla they found just to eat the rest, when they could be purchased for a mere 12 cents per kilo hot off the press at the *tortilleria* in town. Some of the families had fathers who were too embarrassed by their family's circumstances, and they didn't come to the food line. We sent extra food for those dear men doing the best they could in a desperate life situation.

The organization also worked in the orphanages and the Tijuana jail. The jailers didn't feed the inmates that were stacked eight persons to a cell with an open toilet, two dented, rusty metal bunks, and newspapers for blankets. The sustenance of the inmates was left to the families who oftentimes had no resources to even feed themselves. In the orphanage, the nuns barely had time to feed and clothe the children before they'd start with another round of changing babies' diapers.

Aware of the children's need for more human contact, we held and rocked infants a lot—it wasn't uncommon for me to have one in each arm as my foot rocked another child in a bouncer! We also played with the little ones who had nothing to call their own except the shoes on their feet, as all other uniform clothes were communal. A blown-up balloon was met with the greatest wonderment when handed to a child to keep as theirs. We joyfully engaged with all the kids till we had to depart to get back across the border, but it was very difficult to leave it all behind, both physically and emotionally.

Many of us continued working stateside on our own to find food and other necessities for Mexican families on the knife-edge of existence. We regularly set up tables at a grocery store and handed out leaflets to people as they entered. We asked if they were willing to pick up an item or two from the list and drop it off to us on their way out. Additionally, though we didn't tell our coordinator, we dumpster dove and came up with day-old nutritious items that were foraged from the "trash" but were of better quality than what the families were unearthing with their hunts in the dumps. We made those deliveries on our own time, so the hunger project wasn't associated with our "extracurricular" activities.

Though it was never one of my goals while I worked on the hunger project, I finally felt some personal fulfillment. I was spending my time in a worthwhile way—it was necessary and valuable—not for money or grades or pride, not for parental approval or to please a professor. It felt good because it just felt right in so many ways. My mother later told me she could tell how gratified I felt and was concerned I wouldn't come back East and finish my degree—and I had just one semester left!

Openly admitting he was on a mission to make sure I *did* return East, my boyfriend of the previous three years, Dave, came out to visit me during that fall semester in San Diego. Tall and handsome with a shock of curly hair, an endearing crooked smile, and beautiful, sad eyes, Dave had been raised in the upper-class lifestyle of Shaker Heights, Ohio. We were seemingly opposites in almost everything we did. In fact, he was everything I wasn't in that he was a bit rebellious due to his upbringing while I was highly compliant. His father was a company CEO who focused primarily on appearances; getting good grades, looking a certain way, and heading to a good college were highly important to him. You needed to be on track to a life of financial success. Individuality or personal sensibilities were of secondary concern.

For instance, Dave wanted to wear his hair long like every other teen in 1970, but his father was adamantly opposed, and he drove Dave to his conservative barber to take care of the "problem." Though he doesn't recall the content, the lecture on the car ride convinced Dave that his dad didn't care about him or how he felt, only his appearance. When they arrived, he wordlessly got out of the car and started to walk back home, his face set like flint. His father didn't bother to notice all the emotion involved; instead, he just drove away. Later, his dad announced at the dinner table that he would no longer look at his oldest son's face until he cut his hair. Sadly, it would take many years.

He was such a smart, athletic, well-rounded person, but when he was in high school, he had no recall of his family's support. He diligently worked and achieved Eagle Scout, the highest Boy Scout rank, with no parental involvement. He was a state champion defenseman hockey player and only recalls that his mom came and anxiously watched through the threaded fingers of her hand-covered face, fearing for his safety. (Although I loved hearing the story of when my proper, Southern-lady mother-in-law got indignant because someone yelled, "Kill number five!" [her son], and she straightened them out!) As a junior, he received the highest accolade for a singer when he was rated the best tenor soloist in the entire state of Ohio, but his parents were not present. Dave was a wonderful sailor, but he chose to race the Great Lakes on a different boat from his father's, with another crew, because his dad didn't accept input from his long-haired son, even when he was the superior sailor. Thus, I came to understand why he had those beautiful, sad eyes I loved so much.

For most of his childhood, Dave's siblings also treated him differently. His sister, only 18 months younger, and another brother, who was five years younger, in all likelihood have vivid memories of the tension in the house without a distinct understanding of its origin. The youngest brother would likely have no memory of that fateful dinner; he just knew Dave was treated differently—separate. They were all sadly unaware their father was working feverishly at appearances because he was trying to create an aura of respectability after experiencing his own difficult, complicated childhood. Their dad's upbringing was never a permissible subject for conversation as he always tried his best to bury the past.

From the time he was 13, Dave's dad only addressed him while looking him in the chest and never at his face. Conversations no longer took place at all, even into Dave's adulthood. Sadly, the divisive declaration of the father caused him to lose the respect of his son, and the rebellion began.

Dave intentionally stayed away from his family so he wouldn't feel like he was being treated like the odd man out. He did what his father expected and then did whatever he wanted as well. He got great grades—and smoked pot. Dave was an acolyte at church but was often hungover and closed his eyes while leaning back into a niche on the altar right in the middle of Sunday service. However, he got into the Naval Academy, and his dad was delighted and wanted him to attend. He even offered him any car of his choice if he'd go, but Dave was resolute in his decision. Sight unseen, he headed for Bowdoin College in faraway Maine to get excellent grades for his dad, and party, play hockey, and sail for himself.

Dave and I on the roof of the cabin awaiting a meteor shower the first summer we dated, 1980.

Trisha's Tangent

As a parent, I understand Dave's dad. He was simply trying to command what was in his realm of control—himself. But parents have to learn to focus on what's most important—and something as temporary as hair length *should not* be considered as important. By erecting a wall between them over this trivial issue, it painfully became a watershed moment in Dave's childhood. Later, when his hair was short, Dave became successful in business, respected as a church elder, had a happy marriage, and raised a big family. It must have just seemed too late for his dad to rectify the mistake, to heal the division, and he never did.

I met Dave after he selected Bowdoin College, in my New England home turf, and ultimately, our relationship began. We started to date at the end of my freshman year when he was a senior, and he got grief for robbing the cradle. He had mellowed quite a bit by then, and we joked that we wouldn't have had anything to do with each other when we were in high school—the bad boy vs. the goody-two-shoes daughter of a cop.

Dave had grown up without his father's input and now wanted to do life differently, especially to have an active relationship with his own family someday. I respected that. He intended to make sure his family knew they were unconditionally loved and would attend all the games, concerts, and all the other life events important to his children.

Now, back to Dave's trip to San Diego during my senior year of college. During his visit, he proposed marriage to me. I wanted to shout, "Yes!" as I loved him completely, but I needed to figure out the next step of my life. As a senior, I was in a dither trying to figure out what lay ahead and needed to nail down at least one variable from which to launch my adult life. It would be helpful to know where I'd be and who I'd be with!

But though it could alleviate my anxieties, I didn't feel I should give him an answer until I asked him a serious, life-altering question. Having spent so much time with the orphans on the hunger project, I knew I wanted to walk down the path of adoption someday, and he needed to know about this before we could make a life plan together. So, I didn't give him an answer right away.

Dave told me how heart-wrenching it was for him to wait several days for my response, but shortly thereafter, I took him down to Tijuana. I showed him the dire circumstances and told him of my heartfelt desire to adopt someday—not because I couldn't or wouldn't have children but because such a great need had to be filled. Dave's heartstrings were pulled like mine, and he immediately agreed. Once we agreed on adoption, I joyfully accepted his proposal, and we became officially engaged.

Then, with great difficulty, I pried myself away from the Southern California sunshine and my beloved hunger project, returning to New England at the end of the semester with the hope to return to adopt someday.

Trisha's Tangent:

Look Back to Move Forward

Look at your own life. When things in your life feel clearly "right" to you, it can be a strong indication of how God has built you and the purpose He has created you for. When you seek Him for your purpose, always look back, even if you didn't know Him at the time, and look for such truths about yourself. There are hints to the "how" and the "why" questions of your life—the purpose for which you were created.

The next spring, I graduated from Bowdoin College, and in the summer of 1983, Dave and I were married in my quaint hometown, Melrose, Massachusetts.

My dad called me "Trisha Transition" throughout this eventful season because I went from being a student to a teacher, a player to a coach, a penniless student to a car- and homeowner, a Bostonian to a Clevelander, and single to married. For your mental health, therapists and psychologists say you really shouldn't do more than one, maybe two, of these big life events in a given year. I loved Dave, but I was losing my grip on my controlled life during this period. I no longer had religion or any other stabilizing force.

Though we had settled into work and married life in Ohio, I was reeling from the myriad of changes that had occurred to me in such a short time. I felt like I was carried along by a swift, threatening current and thought that I'd be able to stand if only I could get a grip on *something*. As I sought stability, I doubled down on my ongoing search for peace and truth. For years, Dave had been tolerant of my odyssey, and though curious, he never chose to join my quest.

He was raised in the straitlaced Episcopal Church in northeast Ohio. This particular denomination presented to me as "Catholic-lite"; vestments and liturgy, points in the service where you stand, kneel, sit—all the usual stuff for religion in a mainline denomination church.

I felt like the Catholic religious life was over for me as I believed I'd "grown" beyond it through my spiritual explorations. I'd created my own belief system and been freed from the Catholic "religious, guilt-ridden stuff" I thought was part of my problem. This left a hole in my life, which I was trying to fill with answers to my endless list of questions. My search seemed to only increase the volume of questions as one world religion after another contradicted themselves. So,

I started to take pieces from each of them that resonated with me, stitched them together, and made my own patchwork quilt of beliefs.

But Dave and I felt our children needed *some* sort of religious foundation from which they would grow. We had three small children within six years of our wedding with the intent to have our biological kids before adoption. We decided to go with "Catholic-lite" because I didn't want to backpedal all the way to Catholicism. So, we began to attend a local Episcopal church, which was similar but smaller than the "High Church" congregation from Dave's childhood.

For purely social reasons, I joined a ladies Bible study and began to enjoy reading the content and giving it consideration. I'd never done this before! As a kid, I recalled being afraid to read it. Sometimes I'd open the Bible and slam it shut as if something supernatural would leap out at me!

Dave and I also joined a young couple's Bible study to meet other people our age and in our phase of life. Sadly, I had read so much contradictory religious and irreligious literature over the years while developing my own belief system, and a lot of it confused me. I asked *so* many irksome questions and challenged every subject presented and person who taught it. I was a figurative thorn in each group leader's side as my questions seemed to come *at* them:

Why doesn't ancient Chinese religion account for Jesus?

Why does just one way lead to God? To heaven?

Can't we just do and be the best we can and be accepted? Why is your best not good enough?

Isn't heaven and hell of our own creation?

Our family before the calling came: Dave, me, Daniel, Sarah and Nathan.

Don't a myriad of places in the Bible contradict each other? Why?

How could God be the author? How did He tell someone what to write?

Why does the earth have so much suffering and pain if God is in control?

If reincarnation isn't true, why did Jesus say He'd come again?

The questions were voluminous. I wanted answers, and I *fired* my queries at the Bible study teachers.

Eventually, I got to the point where I just wanted to believe and have faith. But despite my desire to stem the tide of the inquisition, the onslaught of questions would not stop coming forth. There seemed to be an impetus behind the questions, and *that* force was in charge, driving my inquisition onward and unabated.

I continued to go to the studies where I sat quietly and listened to the prayers and petitions of others but with little interest in prayer myself. I lacked trust in the One to whom prayer was aimed; instead, I trusted myself. But then something out of my control happened in what seemed to be our perfect little family. Our sweetheart preschool daughter needed surgery.

Sarah was a bright little porcelain doll with a pretty round face set with big blue eyes and a sweet disposition to match. At the tender age of three, she had developed a dangerously high tolerance for pain after years of chronic ear infections. Yet, she never complained. Once when I took her little brother in for a checkup, the doctor, aware of her ear history, asked to also give her ears a quick look. We were so distressed to find she had double ear infections and walking pneumonia! And she hadn't even made a whimper! After years of struggle, there was a terrible infection that caused a nasty burst eardrum, and ultimately, Sarah's ear needed surgical repair. I took her to the specialist, and he asked me to sign a paper that stated she could possibly be made deaf or worse by the recommended surgery and that he would not be held responsible.

With anxiety and tears, I relayed this to the ladies at my Bible study, and they told me I should take Sarah to the healing service on Wednesday night. I was hesitant. "I thought it was for cancer and stuff," I said. They assured me that God cared about everything, and I should take her to Him at the healing service. If it were just for me, I'd have skipped it, but for my uncomplaining, long-suffering, sweet little daughter and her hearing, I obliged and did as they suggested. No stone was left unturned on behalf of her health and wholeness.

The healing service was in the main sanctuary and a small clutch of people was at the front, as most of the pews sat empty. Sarah grasped my hand in hesitation—feeling defensive myself, I picked her up and tucked her on my hip. Sheepishly, we went down the carpeted center aisle, and I haltingly stated why I had come. I fully expected them to turn me away and tell me to come back when I had a *real* issue or a life-threatening case, but they didn't. When everyone was seated in the pews, they went through a number of scriptures about Christian healing promises in the Bible and Jesus's ministry to the sick:

The prophet Isaiah said of the Messiah to come;

'But he was pierced for our transgressions;

he was crushed for our iniquities;

upon him was the chastisement that brought us peace;

and with his wounds we are healed."

(Isaiah 53:5)

"Therefore, confess your sins to one another and pray for one another, that you may be healed."

(James 5:16)

After several more scriptures to build up people's faith about God's will to heal, each person went forward to the altar for individual prayer by the elders (James 5:14). When it was her turn, they anointed Sarah's head and laid hands on her as I held her. They declared a specific scripture over her:

"The hearing ear and the seeing eye, the Lord has made them both."

(Proverbs 20:12)

Then they prayed for God to make Sarah's ears *perfect*. I was highly doubtful because this child had never had "perfect" ears—better was just fine, but wouldn't perfect be great? Could it be possible? Apparently, God was undeterred by my doubts and unbelief because even though it wasn't evident at that particular moment, He did a miracle in our daughter's ears.

The very next day I took Sarah to the pediatric ENT (ear, nose, and throat specialist) for her final checkup before her scheduled Friday surgery. Using his otoscope, he peered in her ears, then furrowed his brow and gave me a puzzled look, then back to his scope to check her ears again. As the doctor exhaled with a bit of a harrumph, he said, "I don't understand it. If I'd never seen these ears before, I'd say there had never been a problem! There is no scarring and not even any residue from the blood. They're perfect!"

I was stunned. He repeated what *the elders* had said at the church service! God healed her and made her ears *perfect*. After I tried to explain the inexplicable—about the previous night's prayers and the healing service—the skeptical, dismissive doctor sent us home and canceled Sarah's surgery.

My mind was blown.

God could make things perfect?!

I needed to think.

I needed to call Dave.

I needed to talk to my Bible study leader.

And I needed to pray!

The next week, with thankful tears of joy, I relayed the whole healing story to my Bible study group. They were abuzz with gratefulness to God for what He had done, and they likely continued to pray for this wayward young mom because I *still* had yet to see the whole truth about what Jesus came to do—because it wasn't just to heal my little girl's ears!

One night, shortly thereafter, I woke to the sound of the word "Job" and, later in the week, the line "in Him there is no darkness at all." After I received God's poetic salvation invitation, "The Correction,"* followed by a tearful reading of the book of Job, clarity dawned, and massive conviction came down on me like a ton of bricks—like a very *gentle* ton of bricks. I may well have been reading God's book, but He was most certainly reading my mail!

Then the Lord answered Job out of the whirlwind and said: "Who is this that darkens counsel by words without knowledge? Dress for action like a man; I will question you, and you make it known to me.

"Where were you when I laid the foundation of the earth? Tell me, if you have understanding. Who determined its measurements—surely you know! Or who stretched the line upon it? On what were its bases sunk, or who laid its cornerstone when the morning stars sang together, and all the sons of God shouted for joy?

"Or who shut in the sea with doors when it burst out from the womb, when I made clouds its garment and thick darkness its swaddling band, and prescribed limits for it and set bars and doors, and said, 'Thus far shall you come, and no farther, and here shall your proud waves be stayed'?

"Have you commanded the morning since your days began, and caused the dawn to know its place, that it might take hold of the skirts of the earth, and the wicked be shaken out of it? It is changed like clay under the seal, and its features stand out like a garment. From the wicked their light is withheld, and their uplifted arm is broken.

"Have you entered into the springs of the sea, or walked in the recesses of the deep? Have the gates of death been revealed to you, or have you seen the gates of deep darkness? Have you comprehended the expanse of the earth? Declare, if you know all this.

"Where is the way to the dwelling of light, and where is the place of darkness, that you may take it to its territory and that you may discern the paths to its home? You know, for you were born then, and the number of your days is great!

"Have you entered the storehouses of the snow, or have you seen the storehouses of the hail, which I have reserved for the time of trouble, for the day of battle and war?" (Job 38:1-23)

What was this?!

Who *do* I think I am to question God on how He does His things? How arrogant could I be?!

But He heard me ... knew me ... understood me ... and loved me anyway!

I felt like a child being chastised and disciplined by her sweet, caring Father. Prostrating on my dining room floor, I repented with all my sinful heart. He loved me just the way I was but was unwilling to leave me in my state of ignorance and unbelief.

I asked for His forgiveness for thinking I knew it all from my explorations in false world religions. I know the truth *now* because I knew *Him. He* was the truth. I asked Him to do as He saw fit with my life such as it was, and He alone would be glorified by it. I was so humbled and happy—so happy the tears flowed down my *chest* in a steady stream, just like the poem.

I looked at the three stanzas of the poem from God and analyzed them from my new vantage point of faith.

The Correction

Original Sin began at the Fall,

Our nature determined, for each one and all.

Cut off from our God, some way to begin,

Our spirits cut off by Original Sin.

The Lord sent His Son, such mercy has He.

He came as the Savior, for you and for me.

Now Jesus has come, we all can stand tall,

In Him there is no darkness at all.

Reunion with God, we can now complete.

The Sinner's Prayer, we all must repeat.

Ask Christ in your life, He will come in,

Corrected you now, the Original Sin.

---

*Several years later, I titled the poem "The Correction" for two reasons: First, God had handed down a massive correction to me that was needed and welcome. Second, I had made a personal course correction in my life when I gave up the questioning and became a child of faith in the Lord Jesus Christ.

The first stanza told me my problem. My spirit was cut off from God by the original sin of Adam; I contended with rebellion and sin because I had no power over them. They had been part of all human nature since the fall.

"So I find it to be a law that when I want to do right, evil lies close at hand. ...Wretched man that I am! Who will deliver me from this body of death?"

(Romans 7:21, 24)

The second stanza told me God's solution to my problem. He had sent His Son, Jesus, to live a sinless life on earth and then to die in my place for my sin.

"For the wages of sin is death, but the free gift of God is eternal life in Christ Jesus, our Lord."

(Romans 6:23)

"There is therefore now no condemnation for those who are in Christ Jesus. For the law of the Spirit of life has set you free in Christ Jesus from the law of sin and death."

(Romans 8:1–2)

The last stanza told me how to accept God's solution. When I accepted Jesus as my Savior and trusted in His substitutionary death for me, I was saved by God's grace through faith in His Son. It was a gift—no way to merit it, earn it, or work for it. Perfectionism didn't help either; no wonder that path was fruitless for me! I could only correct the original sin by receiving the gift of Jesus as Lord of my life.

"For as in Adam all die, so also in Christ shall all be made alive."

(1 Corinthians 15:22)

"… It is the gift of God, not a result of works, so that no one may boast."

(Ephesians 2:8–9)

Earlier in life, I didn't know about this relational God and this spiritual side of life because the practice of religion kept me blind. Arriving here and finding God proved to be quite an odyssey for me—not because He didn't want to be found but because I didn't see the truth till I first looked in all the wrong places.

I discovered He is a personal God who cares and understands, takes time to talk to His children, heals, corrects, and loves His children—one at a time or in groups or by nations. He is God—and I am so happy I am no longer Lord of my own life.

The marathon of questions was no longer running through my mind because it had reached the finish line. I found out the truth, and it set me free! I no longer needed to do everything right or achieve some ideal. I was loved just the way I was and knew He had everything about my life under control. He always did. Amazingly, He saw the awful depths of my sinful heart and loved me anyway.

Once I found and trusted the One who made me, it cut off the access the devil had to my heart and soul. *Satan* was the impetus behind the inquisition. In hindsight, even though questions are good, I realized the enemy can sometimes fuel them to keep you *from* faith instead of leading you *to* faith. My query had become out of control, but my salvation and conversion stopped the plans the enemy had to destroy me by hanging with my endless rope of questions.

"... Be strong in the Lord and in the strength of His might. ... that you may be able to stand against the schemes of the devil."

(Ephesians 6:10–11)

I knew where I came from and where I was headed. In very short order, God let me know why I was here and why it mattered. What else did I really need to know?

I had been looking for the truth by seeking information, but my conversion showed that God straightened out my search—I was in search of a person, and He revealed Himself! This revelation and His solution to my problem filled the massive God-shaped hole in my life. But He was yet to show me *why* I was here on this earth—and He was about to do just that.

**Call to Me and I will answer you, and tell you great
and hidden things you have not known.**

(Jeremiah 33:3)

2

The Calling

Back then, I didn't realize it, but my salvation story was extraordinary. It was even dramatic. I thought God was doing that kind of thing all the time—revealing Himself in dreams, healing people, overtly telling people His Word. It was all I knew.

Due to the miraculous nature of my conversion, not in a church and with no one but God present, when I eventually read of the apostle Paul, struck blind by God on the road to Damascus, I completely identified with him. It was so consistent with God's initial involvement in my own life.

Paul was separated from God by the legalism of his Jewish faith while believing he was actually serving Him. Paul persecuted God's followers who believed in Jesus and was staunchly headed in the wrong direction. But in my experience, when God knows someone wants the right way and the truth to be made manifest in their life, He moves. Big time. And just like me, Paul was dealt a major course correction (Acts 22:6–16)!

Paul was struck blind and unable to move when God called him to be His apostle to the Gentiles. Similarly, I realized I was weak and unable to do anything of value without God. I felt loved, happy, and humbled but keenly aware of my own inadequacy as I'd finally come to the revelation that He's God—and despite New Age claims, I'm not! But right then, when I felt as useless as blind Paul, God revealed His calling on my own life.

Really God?!

This is how You work?!

I'm completely incompetent!

I know *nothing!*

But what I did know was He alone was the author and creator of all these supernatural incidents in my life. So regardless of the pushback from people, and there were those who thought I'd lost my mind, I did everything possible to cooperate with His plans. I knew I could do nothing, but He could do *anything.*

"I am the vine; you are the branches. Whoever abides in me and I in him, he it is that bears much fruit, for apart from me you can do nothing."

(John 15:5)

God had called me out of my ignorant darkness and into His marvel-
ous light, and He was about to fast-track plans that would make my
life quite exciting and venturesome. And I was ready and willing to
play right into His hand. But first, He had to get Dave on board this
heaven-sent bullet train before it left the station.

Trisha Tangent

I was baptized the month after my conversion in a backyard pool, along with a number of friends from Bible study. I received literature about water baptism, and I shared it all with Dave. He had taken in everything I'd told him about my home conversion but was still in thought, considering all of it in his usual analytical and measured way.

At the baptism, my friend asked where Dave was, and I told her he planned to come and support me. When he finally arrived, he was in swim trunks. He had made his own decision for Christ after God opened his eyes about Jesus when he read a prophecy in Isaiah:

> Surely he has borne our griefs and carried our sorrows; yet we esteemed him stricken, smitten by God, and afflicted. But he was pierced for our transgressions; he was crushed for our iniquities; upon him was the chastisement that brought us peace, and with his wounds we are healed. All we like sheep have gone astray; we have turned—every one—to his own way; and the Lord has laid on him the iniquity of us all. He was oppressed, and he was

afflicted, yet he opened not his mouth like a lamb that is led to the slaughter, and like a sheep that before its shearers is silent, so he opened not his mouth.

(Isaiah 53: 4–7)

Upon Dave's profession of faith, we were baptized together that same night as we held hands in the backyard swimming pool. We went under the water together and emerged as a couple, united in Christ and ready for whatever God had planned.

After his salvation, Dave tried several times to ask forgiveness from his parents. He admitted to his teenage rebelliousness with all humility, but they refused to listen because they wanted to believe he hadn't done the things he confessed. Though for appearances they were civil as adults, his father sadly maintained his posture of disregard toward Dave even to his dying day. He made his daughter, with a hospitality degree, the executor of his will rather than his oldest son, who had been degreed in math and the CFO for a large medical company.

Now that we were saved, baptized, and ready for action, God didn't pause a beat in His expansive plans for our lives. Just weeks after our baptism, in His typical spectacular fashion, God called us to adoption.

He revealed His plans for our family through vivid dreams that involved adopting kids. To me, the dreams felt normal because I'd started my Christian life having been literally awakened by God. I hadn't put Him into any religious box He needed to extricate Himself from before I'd pay attention. I didn't have any theological blockades to tear down in order for Him to communicate with me. He had my full attention, and I knew it was Him.

"My sheep hear My voice, and I know them, and they follow Me."

(John 10:27)

I love God's Word and am committed to His church. However, spiritual experiences can be hard for some people, so I kept a lot of these occurrences to myself, my husband, and a few close friends whom I knew were prayerful believers. After my salvation, I learned that people who weren't ready to hear about God and His will weren't ready to hear *from* Him either. But through several prophetic dreams, God laid down the foundation for a work He had planned from the beginning of my life … our marriage … probably even the beginning of time.

Initially, I didn't know the dreams had to do with adoption, but they were centered on a baby girl named "Danielle," and she was clearly our daughter. She was African American, had one arm, and was a tiny, darling, cheerful little girl. She was of different ages in the dreams but always the same sweet child, and it was obvious she was our daughter.

I couldn't recall the actual events in the dreams, but I awoke with the conviction the little girl was ours. After the third dream, I awoke on a Sunday morning and, as usual, excitedly told Dave about it.

At that time, we were out of town on a business trip and had planned to go to the Episcopal church by our hotel in Naples, Florida. Sunday morning church had become our usual family pattern. We walked into the very full church, sandwiched into a pew with a number of other parishioners, and partook in the typical Episcopalian pattern of worship to which we'd grown accustomed. Then, they got to the Bible readings, and it was like my own mind expanded, as God spoke and everyone else in the church just faded away:

And Jesus took a child and put him by his side and said to them,

"Whoever receives this child in my name receives me, and whoever receives me receives him who sent me."

(Luke 9:48)

At the altar, the priest read quite matter-of-factly, unaware he was being used as an oracle of God. Back in the pew, I started to shake and weep uncontrollably from the very depths of my soul. God was calling us to receive this child, Danielle! The dreams were about adopting!

Dave was frantically searching his mind for why I was in tears, when I showed him the scripture and whispered, "Danielle." I watched the reality dawn on his face and a smile spread across it. He put a comforting arm around me, pulled me close, and kissed my head. God had orchestrated the dreams, the trip, the scripture at the church—all of it. He was indeed now calling us to the life of adoption, in a rather spectacular fashion, leaving no doubt that He was the author of our calling! A few days later, we went home with a keen sense of purpose but had no idea how to move forward with it.

Back in Ohio, we relayed the contents of the dreams to a young pastor friend at the church. Various components made it evident we were to seek a transracial, special needs adoption. He went on to pray for clarity about how we were to move forward. The problem was that we couldn't just call an agency and make inquiries about the specificities of children in their care! It would go over like a lead balloon:

"Yes, hello. We were wondering if you have any African American baby girls in your care *with one arm*."

We prayed about it and boldly decided to just start trying to proceed in the process. After a lot of phone calls to local agencies, we even looked into international adoption as we couldn't determine Danielle's origin just from her appearance in the dreams. We thought of Tijuana but knew she wasn't likely to be Mexican. She could be from the United States, but she could also be from an African nation, a Caribbean Island, or from any number of other countries.

Another problem was that most of our agency inquiries were met with suspicion—why would a couple with three healthy young children seek to adopt a child of color with special needs? Social workers were typically polite but then told us to go home and just enjoy our kids. Of course, I'd told no one the story about the Danielle dreams—it was the better part of wisdom since I knew unbelievers would think I was a fool or plain crazy. They may have sent us home *and* called Children's Services to check on our psychological fitness as parents!

Shortly thereafter, I started to get a nudge from God to speak with a certain woman at our church who was a well-known busybody. I often avoided her to keep myself from hearing her gossip or becoming a party to her latest rumor! At first, I wondered if it was God, but He was persistent like the line of scripture that woke me in the night. He was insistent; "Talk to her!" So, I resolved in my heart to speak with her at the next after-church coffee hour, the one place our lives intersected.

As God intended, it came on the very next Sunday. I braced myself, took a deep breath, walked right up to her, and asked the open-ended question, "So, Joan,* how are things with you?" She told me a couple of anecdotes. Thankfully, none of it was gossip-laden, and then she reciprocated the question. I took another deep breath and plunged in with what God had called Dave and I to do. At the end of my tale of not knowing how to proceed in this calling, she said, "I don't know if you know this, but I am on the county board for unwed teen mothers."

I just smiled to God—He *is* omniscient—He truly does know *everything*!

Joan proceeded to say she knew the National Association of Black Social Workers (it's a real thing, I promise) was making it exceedingly difficult to place Black children in White homes. But she *also* knew a particular social worker who chose to "swim upstream against that particular current," and she promised to speak with her the next time their paths crossed.

The *next day*, the social worker sat down next to Joan at a board luncheon. Our story was fresh in her mind, and she shared our desire to seek a transracial, special needs adoption. The social worker gave Joan her business card, and she happily said she'd be expecting our call.

When she arrived home from her luncheon, Joan called me, sounding all excited with her update. I quickly got off with a hearty thank-you for her help and then prayed. I asked God to surround me with favor

---

*Name has been changed for privacy.

when I called the social worker. Quite eager, though nervous, I tremulously made the life-altering phone call.

We spoke just a short time, but the social worker made her professional opinion plain: 85% of the children in foster care are non-Caucasian, and 85% of adoptive families *are* Caucasian; until more non-Caucasian adoptive families stepped forward, she would continue to place children of color (Black, Hispanic, Asian, Native American, etc.) in White homes rather than place them in long-term foster care. Would Black homes and families be best for Black kids? Of course. But the statistics just can't support seeking to achieve that end. I loved her big, wonderful, and wise social worker's heart from that very minute!

She worked for a Catholic agency, and I was concerned that since we weren't Catholics, it might be a problem. It was not. We went through the usual arduous adoption process with mountains of paperwork and a thorough home study. Every corner of our lives was delved into by social workers—financial, psychological, educational, social, and family history. I even had doctors fill out extensive medical questionnaires—for all five of us!

After the reams of paperwork, we were accepted as a family waiting for placement. As all adoptive families, we got to experience the crazy emotional rollercoaster of having the phone ring and thinking we were getting a child placement, but then we were told a birth mom made a different family choice. The social worker assured me that the birth moms didn't always give cogent reasons for her decisions. One birth mom interviewed us, and we really hit it off, but the social worker later confided she had chosen different parents for her child because she liked the woman's shoes (excuse me, she what?!) and was convinced her child was going to be a "snappy dresser." Choosing a mother and father for your child based on a pair of shoes was just far beyond my realm of comprehension, so I decided to stop trying to figure out what the birth mothers wanted. I left it in God's most capable hands.

As He intended, just a few months later (faster than a pregnancy!), we brought home a bouncing baby boy named Zachariah. The agency felt we were the best choice for him because he wasn't a newborn, but a 10-month-old baby, and we had already experienced early childhood with our three biological children. They knew we understood developmental needs better than a family who had yet to experience parenthood and babies. He was multiracial (Black/White/Native American) and the biological child of two unfortunate teenagers who grew up with no parental guidance whatsoever. They were from chaotic, troubled families where addiction and violence were the norm.

It was a difficult transition (see "Trisha Tangent: Transition" below), and we still did it slowly because Zachariah had been in the same foster home since birth and was quite attached to his foster parents. They absolutely loved him, but due to their middle age, they felt he wouldn't get the same childhood opportunities unless he had younger parents and siblings.

The roughest part for me was that his foster parents were chain smokers. If they weren't actively smoking, a cigarette was poised in the ashtray, smoke twirling and ready for the next drag. I brought Zach home on his transition visits and gave him an immediate bath and changed his clothes. Consistent with his household situation, he was having some breathing issues, especially when he had a cold.

He was also very demanding. The baby wanted to be held by me *all* the time; he required lots of reassurance. If I needed a break or just a shower, he'd scream till he was given back to me. But our kids were great about it. They realized he was upset and hurting. We had intended to name him John Albert, after our two grandfathers, but due to his age, we decided to keep the name his foster family had given him—he'd have one less adjustment during the massive household and family changes.

We finally made the permanent break from his first home when we noticed Zach started becoming confused at the end of his visit with us, especially when I tried to leave him back at the foster home. He was gradually forming a strong attachment with our family but still loved and lived with his foster family, which prompted the social worker to make the difficult call, and we made the break complete. It was so hard for the foster parents and their adult children, but the social worker said it was the best thing for Zachariah. It took a while, but we finally settled into a new routine at the Campbells', now a family of six.

Trisha Tangent:
Transitions

When you adopt, the period of time called "transition" takes place when you go back and forth between the foster home and the future adoptive home. This process is designed to give the child time to adjust.

When a child is taken into foster care, such a transition doesn't take place—usually due to a bad situation that required the intervention of Children's Services. The child has to leave abruptly, which is detrimental to their psyche. But despite the unhealthy family situation, it's *that child's* situation—it's their home, their parents, and they love them. But with adoptions, there is time to allow a smoother "transition" for the child.

Unfortunately, change of any kind, whether good or bad, is hard for children. For this reason, Dave and I later changed our adoptive family status to become "foster to adopt" parents. When you have your foster license and are prepared to adopt, you can reduce the number of traumatic changes a child has to endure.

For instance, when we later got our son Sean, he was still designated as a foster child in "temporary custody" because the county had not gotten him to the adoptable status of "permanent custody." When he finally reached that status, two years after we got him, he didn't have to move to a different home. He was already *in* an adoptive home, bonded and secure in his family.

If he were in a "foster only" home, he would have been given an adoptive placement and would have started his transition to the next home. He'd have started all over again, but his sense of belonging, self-worth, and permanency would be disrupted and potentially never recovered due to his age.

But even after we had transitioned Zachariah, the sense something wasn't quite right reared its head again. So, I did what I'd become accustomed to whenever I felt anxious or had an unsure tremulous feeling. I went on my knees and prayed.

God showed me baby Danielle was still coming. Zachariah was a transracial, special needs adoption, but he was just represented by the child in the dreams. The *actual* child, Danielle, was still yet to come!

My next concern was how I was to tell Dave about it. Our family plate was already very full! So, I decided to just confess my convictions to him and told him I thought baby Danielle was still coming. He just smiled at me like a Cheshire cat and admitted he was in complete *agreement*! Dave also felt the Lord had given him the same sense—she was still yet to come into our family. We chose to keep this truth close to our hearts and trusted God to lead us to the next step as He had done before. We had total faith in Him.

A few months later, when Zach was 13 months old, my friend Joy*, a pastor's wife, called and told me that she'd had a dream that we had a baby girl.

Shut up, I thought.

I proceeded to tell her that we thought Danielle was still out there, and *she* did exclaim, *"Shut up!"*

I'm not kidding.

She went on to argue with me about how busy we already were, stating that the kids were still so young, plus the expense of it all! But when God is involved, your financial situation is irrelevant—the Lord owns the cattle of a thousand hills! (Psalm 50: 10-11) When God gives the

*Name has been changed for privacy.

vision for something, He also gives the *pro*vision for it as well. If He could part the Red Sea, lead a self-sufficient, academic egghead like me to faith and heal my children, He would surely enable us to afford and care for five young children as well. So, we asked that she remain discreet while keeping the whole situation in prayer.

Dave and I began to fast on a regular basis. We prayed and sought God's direction. We had no idea where our baby was, but we knew she was out there!

About a month later, in the spring, I was kind of sad and wondering where Danielle was and if she would look like the baby in my dream—I needed hope and encouragement. It was at this point that the incredible God of details showed up again in an extraordinary way. It was 1993, and in the year prior, God had inspired someone at the Ashton-Drake doll company to make a doll named *Danielle*. I happened upon her picture while in a doctor's waiting room. Nonchalantly thumbing through a magazine, I came upon a porcelain doll advertisement, but the picture was my baby girl from my dream! There she was! And the doll's name was Danielle! I felt guilty, but I carefully tore the page from the magazine and slipped it into the diaper bag wedged next to me in my seat.

My baby! She was an African American baby girl with one sock on while holding the other one—and she looked exactly like the baby from my dream!

This kind of "coincidence" is what I like to call a "seam-binding" incident. God knows so many details, far more than we could ever imagine, let alone keep track of; He is the orchestrator and conductor of *everything*. The reason I call His detailed incidences seam-binding moments is due to a passage I found in the book of Exodus. God gives minute specifics about the priest's garments and in His description, He includes *seam binding* on the neck of their robes. As a seamstress, I knew this was to keep the weight of the piece from tearing and to make sure it is comfortable for the priests. God cares so much for each one of us, and He even cares if we are comfortable!

He knows us better than we know ourselves, and He knows our needs before we can even think to ask. God was aware I required some kind of visual encouragement to keep the faith while not knowing where baby Danielle was or when she'd arrive. He graciously knew I'd need another faith lift in what I call the "mean time," between the promise and His fulfillment.

Spring marched on, summer arrived, and we were scheduled to go on another business trip, this time to Sausalito, California. At that time, when Dave and I needed to go out of town, we had a young couple, "Miss Nancy" and "Mr. John," who brought their older kids to *our* house to make life easier for all our young children. Our kids had their own toys and beds, plus they didn't have to pack up and move. This was the easiest way we could handle long-term childcare for four small children, ages one, three, five, and seven.

Unfortunately, an emergency arose for Nancy and John, so they had to call off, and I could do nothing to replace them. They were irreplaceable. Finding care for four little ones on short notice was really impossible. Sadly, I bowed out of the trip that was to include California sunshine and an expedition to their wine region, Sonoma and Napa Valley. But it was for a divine purpose, and God alone knew at the time.

During Dave's solo week away, the phone rang, and it was Joy, the same friend that had the baby girl dream a few months earlier. Joy was an inner-city nurse with a big heart for the underprivileged, and she was a wonderful physician. More precisely, she was a nurse practitioner, and for all intents and purposes, she also did the same things as the doctors. On the phone, she seemed quite manic and started to speak very fast, so I had to stop her and ask her to slow down and start over with whatever she was trying to tell me.

She recounted to me, at that very minute, she had a young mom in her office and was doing checkups on her three stair-step children, who were born just a year apart from each other. As she examined the youngest, the baby was seated on the mom's lap for comfort and security. During her routine exam, Joy brushed the mom's somewhat distended abdomen, and she exclaimed, "Oh my gosh, you're pregnant again?!" The young mom said, "It's not my baby." Joy was perplexed.

Up to this point, it was a normal daily examination room conversation for Joy, which always included discussion of the difficulties of poverty and single parenting. The young mother went on to explain her predicament but uncharacteristically concluded her sad tale; she said she knew she needed to handle life better for her kids to have a decent future, so she needed to stop getting pregnant. She was in such dire straits, she confided that she often ran out of diapers before the end of the month and had to put her babies in double rubber pants! (Whoa! She *was* desperate.) Then she asked Joy if she knew anyone who *wanted a baby girl!* As soon as she said "baby girl," the whole dream from months before flooded forward in Joy's mind. She abruptly excused herself from the room, went out, and called me.

Me. The young mom who happened to be home because she had been recently removed from her husband's business trip. Coincidence? Nope!

During our phone call, Joy said the young mom was unfamiliar with how adoption worked, and with all innocence, was asking people she knew if they wanted a baby girl. She thought someone else could just take her child home from the hospital and raise her as their own with no legal process at all. Additionally, Joy further explained that the mom was too poor to even afford a telephone (this was pre–cell phone days) and she wouldn't be able to get any contact with her after she left the office. Good thing I was home!

I gave her a phone number for a private adoption agency I was familiar with—they had a toll-free 800-number for clients who were very needy and living on the brink of destitution. I told Joy that the mom could use the number anytime, and I also let the agency know that she'd call soon. They could help her with food, maternity clothes, and anything else she needed to be healthy during her pregnancy.

This was why our childcare fell through—it was all about Danielle! God was in control and on the move. Pumped with adrenaline, I excitedly called Dave in California and relayed the incredible story of all that had transpired with our friend Joy. I tried so hard to remember every small detail of the miraculous situation, but I made a hash of it the first time through. After I calmed my emotions a bit, I relayed each minute detail in the correct order. Then, Dave and I prayed together and knew God would show His hand and all we needed to do as His plan for our growing family continued to unfold.

The next month had a lot of commotion as we prepared to bring another little one into the house. The private agency kept the baby from going into "the system," but we had to pay the expenses. We knew from our previous adoption how hard it was to extricate a child if she were to enter the child welfare system, so we chose to keep her adoption private.

We got a wonderful social worker, Ann, from the agency, and she was a Christian believer. It was much easier and more comfortable to have a caseworker with our same values. As part of the intake, the agency visited with the birth mom to check on her health and living situation. Ann told me she was a good mother as she did the best she could in a very difficult predicament since she was financially strapped. Her apartment was tattered and worn, but she always kept it clean. She took her kids to free food programs and to the library for story times. She was aware that reading and education were as important as food; she did her best to parent her children well.

As Ann shared her experiences about her birth mom visit, I was able to reciprocate and told her all about the dreams and what God was doing in our family. It was liberating to have a free and open discussion with a social worker who was a Christian believer. She asked our plans for the baby's name because she was wondering about the close similarity with our oldest son's name, Daniel.

Dave and I discussed the baby's name and how to honor the dream. Then, we decided to use Danielle as her middle name. We prayed and came up with two names, Olive and Esther. Ultimately, we decided the combination "Esther Danielle" sounded best, plus she would have two strong biblical names, boding well for her future.

In addition to all the adoption paperwork, I began to use a hospital grade breast pump to try to bring in my milk again. I had read in one of my adoption books that when a woman has already been a nursing mom, stimulation and demand could get the lactation system back up and running. Since we knew she would be a newborn, we wanted her to have the best possible start in life, including nursing. It was worth a try! The pump was painful and arduous, but well worth the effort for our daughter's health.

A short month later, the tiny baby girl was born full term and healthy. We were elated. When Ann called to tell me the news, she said she had previously been trying to get a hold of me for days. Curious, I asked her, "Why? What's been going on?"

She proceeded to tell me she had found out the birth mother's middle name was Danielle! "*WHAT?!*" I shouted into the phone. I was blown away. There goes my seam-binding God again! Details, details, details!

Ann asked if she could share with the birth mother, and I told her she *absolutely* could tell the mom the baby's middle name was going to match hers—it could give such peace and confirmation she was doing the right thing for her baby.

The agency took custody at birth and placed Esther Danielle in a foster situation to finish all the paperwork and tie up legal loose ends. During those few days of foster care, the birth mom insisted she didn't know the name of the birth father. She was forcing us into a difficult situation because we needed that name for the adoption to proceed in a legal manner. We had to press her on the subject because it was necessary to do a legal "diligent search" for the birth father to fully release Esther for adoption. We knew, based on her demeanor and responsibility as a mom, that she was not the type to have no idea who the father of her child was, and we needed her to give us that name so the placement couldn't be overturned at a later date by the return of a putative father.

With much anxiety, I told the social worker to inform her that she would lose her adoptive family if she didn't give his name. According to Ohio law, if a child is not able to remain with his or her parents, agencies are required to conduct a diligent search for identified relatives and notify them within 30 days of the child's removal so that they can be considered as a placement. It caused a great deal of anxiety, but in the end, she did give the father's name. Thank God, the adoption placement proceeded to completion.

We had the search done and nothing came of it—no birth father was out there looking for this baby. Then we realized what God had shown us by the one-armed imagery in the three dreams. In each one, Esther Danielle only had a single left arm, though in reality, she was born with both limbs healthy. The arms *represented* what people naturally have two of—parents. She had only one biological parent, her mother, which meant only one arm. In the Bible and other ancient texts, the right arm is associated with the masculine side of life. So, Danielle's single left arm represented her mother, but her missing right arm represented her biological father. And we could be at peace with the whole difficult situation because the one-armed dream meant God *knew* she would come to us without a father.

But God blessed Esther with a great dad! Though Dave had to first endure a lecture from his father about how we'd "never get into a club," our whole family went to the agency to pick up our new baby daughter, who was now six days old due to delays from the legal search. Dave's mom came in support of our decision, despite her husband's protestations. My parents had to endorse our decision from afar as they were retired and still living in Maine.

Our new baby daughter was impossibly tiny in our eyes at just five pounds compared to Nathan, our last newborn, who weighed a whopping 9 pounds 11 ounces. She had us at hello and was a beautiful little fruition of God's big promise.

In hindsight, I could see how God had started this particular adventure early in my life as He brought me along to receive the calling to have a multiracial family. When I grew up in my middle-class Caucasian Boston suburb, my family had been close friends with a multiracial one. My mother and a neighbor had gone to their home to welcome them the day they moved in from Detroit, Michigan. I recall some discussion by the adults in my life—they didn't want the new neighbors to feel unwelcome or different, but I didn't understand why. I was only 12.

At the time, Boston was going through forced desegregation and bussing—my policeman father was in full riot gear on a regular basis.

Paul, Helen, Amy and Etsie ready for a 1970s wedding.

It was a time of massive unrest around the subject of race in the late 1960s and early '70s. The father of this multiracial family was Black and politically connected—active and involved in the fight for Civil Rights. He had met his blue-eyed, blond Caucasian wife, Amy, when they were in Volunteers in Service to America (VISTA), a domestic type of Peace Corps. Our families were super close—more like family than some of our biological family. We went to church together, had Christmas Eve together, and went on vacation together as well. Plus, I was one of the primary babysitters for the family. I was with their three boys on a regular basis at the park, at the store, and all over town.

You don't ever accept judgmental attitudes and people's scowled expressions, but I did learn to ignore them and remain happy, loving, and wise when I needed to handle those types of situations. Later,

Foreman Boys: John, David and Daniel.

when I worked on the hunger project in Mexico, I had the same disposition of love and acceptance without regard to socioeconomic status, race, creed, or color.

My purpose was given a foundation by God early in life, even before I decided to seek the truth about Him. Look at your own life—look for atypical things that have happened and see if God was doing something in your heart and mind, even from the earliest time in your life.

Another thing to watch for when you seek your purpose are the things that really *bother* you.

What makes you upset when you see it on the news?

What makes you very *angry*?

What *saddens you*?

These can give you clues to how God created you for a certain kind of purpose.

For me, nothing made me angrier or sadder than child abuse and neglect. If I ever saw a story of want or harm on the news or in the paper, I'd feel the pain and would want to fix it. Similarly, prejudice could get my hackles to rise. That someone could be mean or abusive to someone based solely on their skin color or heritage was abhorrent to me. What matters is what's on the inside of a person, not the outside!

God equips you with the demeanor and experiences you need to fulfill His purpose in your life. We have had to endure hardships from ignorant people, but it is part of the calling. Unkind words and even judgmental body language from people are all part of the course. Our family was under construction to be an example to the world of what He wants—children valued and accepted regardless of race or disability. Though this part of the adoption adventure is difficult, it's meaningful and causes us to grow in patience, love, and forbearance.

Trisha Tangent:
And the Greatest of These Is Faith

When God is ready to do something big in your life, He will increase your faith because you will need it! He built our trust in Him, our reliance on Him, and our faith in Him to such a degree that we just knew that we *knew* He was in control of everything. Our pastor used to say, "When you know in your 'knower.' "

We learned not to fuss about details when He called us to do something. We just moved ahead and trusted Him to put it all in place, to provide for our needs, and continue to fortify our faith. For example, when we were in the valley of decision about the adoptions, He sovereignly healed each of our three biological kids. I mentioned Sarah's ears earlier, but our sons Daniel and Nathan were healed as well.

Our oldest son, Daniel, was a bit of an adrenaline junky his whole childhood, and we had to take him on numerous trips to the emergency room. One day, he came into the house holding his arm at an odd angle, not even crying, and just matter-of-factly said, "I broke my arm again." I asked a couple of questions right away:

Did you hear a crack sound? "Yes."

Do you feel electrical zings to your fingers? "Yes."

I had walked this road with him before and discovered that the bone wasn't dislocated. So, I went to the garage and picked up a length of wood and a saw to fashion a board into a splint. Then, I covered it with duct tape so he wouldn't get a splinter and ace bandaged it to his arm. (Keep in mind, I'd sat in emergency rooms for hours and then ultimately ended up going to an orthopedic surgeon to have it set and a cast placed on it anyway! This way, I thought I'd cut out the middle-man, the ridiculous amount of time in the ER and the big bill!) The next day, I called his orthopedic doctor who was quite familiar with Daniel and his adventurous athletic propensities. And, by the way, the doc remarked, "Nice splint," when we went for his examination.

But this broken arm had a complicating factor. Daniel was supposed to go on a children's missions trip with his church group in two weeks—into the bush of Panama. When I say "into the bush," I truly mean two hours upriver from civilization—no roads. I didn't want him to travel with a full cast! The doctor said he would cast him, check him in two weeks just prior to his departure, and see how the healing progressed. He thought perhaps he could get by with just a splint. We prayed over his arm and read scripture over him about divine healing and healthy bones (Ps 34:20–21).

Two weeks passed; I took him back in, and the bone was completely healed. Thank God! The doctor was amazed, but cautiously optimistic, and made a splint. He told Daniel to put it on if any pain or problem arose—but he was fine throughout the whole trip and never used the splint!

On the other hand, trips with his little brother Nathan were always more difficult and complicated. Nate was asthmatic from birth to such a degree that he had to be on a nebulizer in order to administer medicine to his lungs every day. Sometimes it was done several times a day.

He'd been hospitalized with breathing issues and pneumonia, plus he had frequent emergency room visits due to respiratory arrests.

One time, I was at the car dealership to get maintenance done on my van. Unbeknownst to me, due to the exhaust from all the vehicles in the repair bay and because I didn't smell it, the air quality was low, even in the distant waiting room. I heard Nathan's respiration start to rattle in distress, so I grabbed all three kids and headed for the garage. I told them to get my van down because I needed to *go*. I *had* to get home to the machine and give him a breathing treatment. Now!

As I drove, I heard the rattle stop, and I looked in my rearview mirror. Nathan started to kick his legs and made no sound at all. He just flailed. In order to make sound, air must move across the vocal cords; he was in full respiratory arrest and getting no air at all.

Fear began to physically climb the stairsteps of my spine, but I had to shake it off as it reached my shoulders. I had to think. I couldn't stop, knowing I had no aid to give since no such thing as a rescue inhaler for a baby even exists!

So, I hit the gas.

As I drove, I turned to Daniel, my biggest kid at five years old, and told him to open a window, get his baby brother out of the car seat, and place him face down on the seat by the rushing air. I took the van up to breakneck speeds ... 50 ... 60 ... 70 mph. The wind's force on Nathan's face caused the instinctive baby reaction to inhale, and thank God, I mercifully heard a rattled croak, which meant he was getting *some* air. I continued down the two-lane country road, now going 80 mph in a 50-mph zone.

As we got closer to civilization and the nearest hospital, I slowed a bit but continued cautiously, even with red lights, blaring my horn as I went. We arrived at the hospital, and I grabbed Nathan from the back and ran through the waiting area into the treatment room they had used in the past when he had an asthma crisis. Poor young Daniel was left in the dust to get his three-year-old sister, Sarah, out of her car seat and into the hospital, which he hadn't done before. It took some effort by the doctors, but they restored the baby's airflow. It was jagged and labored, but he was breathing.

Needless to say, I became hypervigilant. I didn't trust anyone to hear the rattle as early as I could, and this resulted in my bondage to his breathing. I kept Nathan in earshot at all times. And if he was asleep, the baby monitor was turned up high so I could hear it from wherever I was. When I slept, I slept lightly, listening all the while. God alone could set me free from this protective maternal obsession.

Dave finally convinced me that Miss Nancy and Mr. John, our wonderful adult caregivers, could handle Nate's asthma. Meanwhile, Dave wanted me to accompany him on an important business trip. He needed his wife back. I went on the trip with him, not without fear and anxiety, but because I left my baby boy in the hands of our sitters and the Lord. This step of faith on my part moved something in the heavens.

While we were in Florida, I had the third dream about Danielle. At the very same hour, when we accepted God's call to adoption at the Episcopalian church by our hotel, Nathan was sovereignly healed at a church service back in Ohio!

God had to breathe life back into *me* so I was freed from the bondage to Nate's respiration and able to even *think* of moving forward with a bigger family. God healed Nathan and *liberated* me.

Freed from the anchor of asthma, Nathan has gone on to lead a life without a wheeze and lettered in four different varsity sports in high school. Today, he is happy, healthy, and athletic as he and his wife live an active, outdoor lifestyle in Colorado.

These two healings were a couple of instances God used to build our faith. We were headed for the season of adoption. We were to be tried and tested like never before, and God knew we needed faith to trust Him completely.

We were thrilled to have Esther Danielle, our daughter of the heavenly dreams, alive, healthy, nursing well, and in our home. But it was hectic. Five children, eight years and younger—they just needed you for everything: physical, emotional, social, you name it. He was causing me to grow and mature into the woman of God I needed to be and to face years of continued adventures with Him.

Amusing Anecdote

We were preparing to sell a car in the early '90s, and a gentleman came to the door from the newspaper. At the time, there was no internet, so he had arrived to take pictures and get my check and advertisement notice. The poor rotund man was a very unhealthy weight, well north of 400 pounds, maybe more. My four-year-old answered the door in our kitchen while I was nearby, and I showed the man which vehicle to photograph and gave him the script for the notice. My son shut the door, looked at me quizzically, and said, "Did he eat too much butter?"

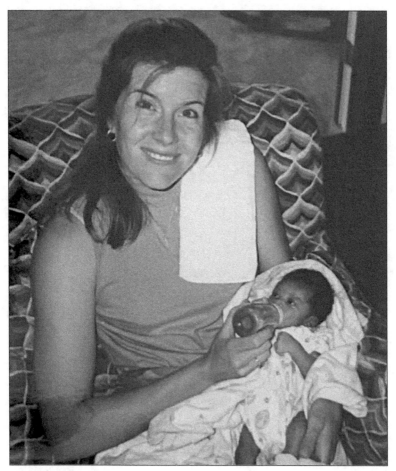

Me with our newborn Ester.

But Noah found favor in the eyes of the Lord.

(Genesis 6:8)

3

We Are Pro Zoe

The next adventure God called us to was a bit chaotic and kind of unnerving. But He alone knew the enormity of the vision we were called to—He was still adding to our brood, so it required expansion of our home too. Maybe this is how unsettled Noah felt when God asked him to build the ark! At the time, we had kids' beds in Dave's home office, and five of them shared a single small bathroom. Growing in our young faith, learning about Christianity and all its facets, Dave and I continued to expect God's unmistakable direction for our family. He highlighted a scripture in Isaiah:

"Enlarge the place of your tent, and let the curtains of your habitations be stretched out; do not hold back; lengthen your cords and strengthen your stakes."

(Isaiah 54:2)]

Still wet behind the ears Christians, we just obeyed Him, hired an architect, and helped design a two-story addition to the house. Included was an office for Dave to replace the one that had been repurposed as a bedroom for kids, plus two more bathrooms and a much-needed children's rumpus room. We also refinanced the house as we felt it would "strengthen our stakes" like the scripture said. But this whole thing required us to step out in financial faith like never before—extra hard for my college sweetheart, a mathematics major.

We were well underway, and the house was a complete disaster area. We couldn't afford to move out during the renovation, so furniture was displaced to all kinds of odd spots around the house like misplaced mannequins in awkward positions. The kids were packed like sardines into the few remaining bedrooms, camping out on the floor like they were on safari. The workers were their guides, and a few of the particularly gruff guys softened and developed a genuine affinity for some of our little boys. They let them "help" when it actually slowed down their work. The boys were quite interested in the power tools and those who operated them!

We woke to zinging circular saws and slamming hammers accompanied by the piquant smell and residue of sawdust and drywall powder, which, despite our best evasive efforts, worked its way into absolutely everything. We probably ate some! Daniel got another broken arm when he jumped from the top of a dresser and tried to swing from a newly exposed rafter. He ended up with a full cast, yet again. I was exceedingly thankful for Nathan's divinely healed lungs, as he kept breathing like a champ despite the effusion of construction debris in the air.

At this time, God was using our domestic construction to work on my own perfectionism issue. Prior to this, I needed to have my home and family the way I wanted it—neat, clean, orderly, and beautiful. As things got "out of hand," He first caused me to be at peace with it and then had me loving the chaos. I was so grateful God had worked the neatnik out of me because I would have found this season far more emotionally arduous. As it was, we endeavored to see it as one more adventure with God.

Then it was time for some large bills to be paid, and we kept walking by faith. Where was it to come from? Though a bit anxious, Dave and I trusted God's provision as in the past.

We had made some serious outlays in construction materials, adoption fees, and caring for our large family, so finances had been very tight. We had two in diapers, ridiculous grocery bills, and oh my gosh, all of the shoes we bought! Kids' feet grow like weeds, and my parents raised me to insist on good quality shoes—feet are important. We also had big bills for hockey equipment and team fees, dance lessons, plus some childhood orthodontia, and now it was holiday time—we couldn't see how we were to afford Christmas gifts for the kids.

Dave said he just didn't know where it would come from ... but God. Miraculously, right *then*, Dave's company decided they *needed* to change when bonuses were given out and moved them up to December in order to be in the same fiscal year.

The company had been growing through mergers and acquisitions, and Dave was in charge of the computer systems integration for all the company changes. The way his mind works makes him a bit of a whiz with information technology. All the transitions were smooth, and the company's board of directors was delighted with the results. They were so pleased with Dave's work they didn't just give him 100% of his goal bonus—they gave him 180%! In the past, they paid out bonuses in March, but we got this mega bonus three months ahead of time, which kept the builder working, paid for Christmas and even allowed us to tithe off the total. God amazed us with His faithful, miraculous provision.

Similarly, we had another financial miracle the next spring. We were to finalize both adoptions, which had large financial balloons payable when the adoptions were completed. Typically, a third is paid when you start the adoption process, another third when a child placement is received, and the last third at the adoption finalization.

We legally completed Esther's adoption down in Columbus, Ohio, because our agency said they are much harder on putative (absentee) fathers than Cleveland. They had done the legal diligent search for Esther Danielle's birth father but wanted to take no chances on the placement being disrupted by his possible return. We had to spend more money on travel, hotel, and meals, but it was well worth it to keep our baby safe from any type of future legal challenge. Then, later that same spring, when it was time to finalize Zachariah's adoption in Cleveland, we went to the courthouse prepared to dig out credit card(s) to make the last payment.

As usual, we arrived a bit early with our five kids in tow, as we didn't want to miss our place in the court's docket. The bailiff called us, and we trooped in with our whole gang: Daniel, Sarah, Nathan, Zachariah, and little Esther, plus our ever-present social worker. The judge was a kind elderly gentleman with out-of-control white hair and a crinkled, cockeyed smile. You could tell he enjoyed this part of his job.

He asked all the kids about their family and their newest little brother. Daniel got a big kick out of going up into the witness stand. Sarah, my shy child, declined the opportunity to go up to the stand but chose to speak confidently and quietly from the comfort and security of her seat beside me. When the court proceedings ended, the judge's gavel came down, and Zach was officially a Campbell. Wahoo! No more social worker visits or getting permission for anything pertaining to our son. No more completion of forms and child status updates. He was just our son!

I turned to our social worker and thanked her for all her work and dedication. Then, I braced myself for the impending cash drain and asked if we needed to make our final payment. The caseworker nonchalantly told us our file was up to date. We even pressed her on it, sure she had made a mistake, so she double-checked. But she insisted our file was up to date financially and in every other way.

"Go home and enjoy your family," she told us. Dave and I just looked at each other in stunned silence; then the light dawned, and we both smiled and gave each other a knowing look that said, "There goes God again!" We had faced a monetary mountain that God must have thrown into the sea for us. Thank You, Lord! We each grabbed a couple of our kids' hands and hustled from the courtroom, off to celebrate Zach's finalization and God's financial deliverance. (Matthew 17:20-21)

We later relayed this story to a pastor friend who showed us in the Bible that God can do a miracle to forgive a debt. He opened to the book of 2 Kings, chapter 6. Some workmen were cutting down trees, and one of them had borrowed an ax.

"But as one was felling a log, his axe head fell into the water, and he cried out, 'Alas, my master! It was borrowed.' Then the man of God said, 'Where did it fall?' When he showed him the place, he cut off a stick and threw it in there and made the iron float. And he said, 'Take it up.' So he reached out his hand and took it" (verses 5–7).

We all know axe heads are not buoyant, but God made iron float—it was a forgiven debt! We could look all we liked, but God had done a miracle and set us free from that monetary obligation, and the bill for the adoption payment had just somehow dematerialized.

This particular miracle made a huge jump in the realm of Dave's trust in God. My husband is gifted with finance and has been a chief financial officer for various companies, as well as governing over information technology and other numerically detailed business practices. God made a big move that required Dave to trust and believe Him for provision when, by the numbers, it looked impossible.

Our family was going to need to trust Him to provide in many arenas where Dave had previously felt he had control. Belief in God's provision for our calling was imperative, and He had made it evident to both of us—we could trust and rest in Him. This was unnerving at first, but we were growing leaps and bounds in our faith through all these adventures with God.

Amusing Anecdote

In addition to the asthma problem, our son Nathan had auditory processing issues due to ear trouble as a little guy. He actually *didn't* get infections, so we were unaware he was having ear issues. I told his preschool teacher he wasn't hearing well, and she felt he was just having "selective hearing" as many little boys do—hear what they want to hear and ignore the rest.

Ultimately, I took him to an ear, nose, and throat specialist after I became convinced he was lipreading. Once, we were doing laundry together, and we started removing clothes from the dryer and putting them into the basket. As we worked, I spoke to him, and since I was facing into the dryer drum, the sound bounced around—though he knew I spoke, he couldn't understand me. He took his little hands, placed them on either side of my face, and turned it toward him. Ah-ha! I was absolutely right! He'd been lipreading! Parents, go with your gut! You may know something is wrong even when you can't put your finger on why!

What had happened in Nathan's predicament was that fluid had entered his ears and solidified. It never infected, so there was no pain to signal us he had a problem. The solidified substance held the tympanic membrane completely still so he could hear sound and intonation but no actual words. The doctor said, "He likely heard what it sounded like on Charles Shultz's *Peanuts* cartoons when the teacher spoke; 'Wa wa waaaa wa waaa wa.' " Upon hearing the doctor's assessment, I proceeded to kick myself around the block. I knew it! Why did I listen to Nate's preschool teacher and wait so long?

He had surgery to remove the solid. Then, they put tubes in the membrane to drain fluid if more were to come into his ear canal, and he was good to go. At least, this was their theory. But he was still struggling with communication post-surgically, and I just knew something *else* still wasn't right. This time, I was proactive and was no longer able to trust others with my son's hearing and his future.

I took him to an audiologist, an actual hearing specialist rather than an ENT, which is an ear health specialist. As it turned out, Nate was hearing, but the part of his brain that processes sound had been taking a circuitous route—receiving from his *visual* line due to years of lip-reading and not his auditory line that runs from the ears.

If an issue like Nate's occurs when the brain is still malleable and developing as a young child, the brain tries to compensate and work around the issue. His auditory processing had actually hardwired to the visual line of Nate's neurology because he was "hearing" by lipreading. Essentially, he had been hearing with his eyes for years.

The doctor said, "Your son literally *sees* what you are saying. For the rest of his life, you will need to make sure he is always front and center in school, sermons, or meetings. He will struggle with picking up 'incidental knowledge,' things that are said and understood by others without being directly said *to* them." Oftentimes, Nate answered even a direct question with "Huh?" Then you had to wait a couple of seconds without saying anything, and the information eventually arrived at the processor in his brain, and he readily answered. Normally, he would hear you but comprehended just a tick slower.

So, life had some pretty amusing moments with this little guy and his auditory delay. For instance, one day in July, when the house was in a flurry of activity, Nate approached me and specifically asked what was up. I told him it took a lot of work to get ready for vacation when you have a big family. He was psyched and exclaimed, "We're going on vacation?!" We had been talking about it at dinnertime for weeks, but no one had picked up that Nate, always attentive to his food, hadn't been jumping into the conversations!

Another funny non-hearing incident was when Nate was being helped into his ice hockey goalie gear. Young hockey players need quite a bit of adult help getting all the gear and skates on correctly, especially goalies. When Nathan was about eight years old, we were late for a game due to rush hour traffic, and I was in the locker room working at a feverish pace to get Nate's goalie pads fastened—making them tight is like wrangling cattle. Two boys were sitting on a bench by us, already geared up, swinging their skated feet, and pondering aloud.

"I think Nate should have to be here early so we don't have to worry about him," one said.

"Yeah, I think so too. I worship Nate; he's the best," replied his teammate.

"You can't do that! It's sacrilege!" exclaimed the first friend.

"I can worship Nate if I want to!" the argument continued.

All this was going back and forth, and Nate never heard a word of it—just working away, putting on his equipment. To this day, he's a humble guy because he rarely hears offhand compliments or admiration from others.

After Dave and I developed our financial trust through the adoptions, God called us to climb out onto yet another unnerving limb—this time with His body of believers. He asked us to leave the comfort of the mainline church, no more Episcopalianism. Because we had both been raised in mainline denominations, it was a bit stressful for Dave and me, but we became part of the founding members of a new non-denominational church right near our home. It was an exciting time.

It was all new—location, pastor, people—and so sweet to have a close-knit, tiny church family. The young congregation was planted when Esther was only six weeks old, and at the end of each Sunday morning service, I had to go find whoever was enjoying their turn holding her. We met in the unremarkable community center of a small nearby town.

We had an undependable old cube truck, and it held all the parapher-nalia of the church. The founding member families arrived early for the chaotic setups on Sunday mornings. We had to put together the sound system for worship, which included a somewhat out-of-tune old upright piano rolled over from its usual home in the corner and a single microphone with low-quality speakers. We just made a joyful noise to the Lord!

Additionally, we had to arrange all the creaky vintage metal folding chairs in the big, drafty civic room with a time-worn old parquet floor. Vintage 1970s gold-colored pinch pleat drapes hung in the windows and held the smells of decades of weddings, charity events, and rotary club meetings. Our pastor's pulpit was an old faux-wood laminate-ve-neered podium with an integrated speaker that may or may not have worked in the past two decades—he just used the worship leader's mic. We put up a sandwich board out front with the church's name and BOOM! We were open.

God's people don't need a big, fancy hi-tech building because where two or more gather in His name, there He is (Matthew 18:20)! We also met at our home on Sunday evenings (remember this detail for later), so we were very thankful for the new house addition. Our big family needed the space, but so did the family of God!

One morning, I was in my walk-in closet praying for my new church and our pastor. My closet was a place of peace and solitude before our motley crew of kids awoke. Without using a dream, God revealed His next step with the Campbells. He made it exceedingly obvious that He was sending another child.

A very specific child because God had a specific message:

"Remember Olive?" the Lord asked me.

"Yes," I replied, "the name I didn't pick for Esther."

"No, she is your next child," He said.

God proceeded to show me He was bringing Olive into our family. *And* He showed me the three kids' names spelled the word *ZOE*— **Z-O-E***.

He made Himself unmistakably plain. "You will stand for the right to life even when you cannot open your mouth to do so. You will be what I want to be instead of abortion."

The wind was knocked out of me, and it felt like the head rush was going to cause a cranial explosion. I shook with the clarity of it. This was another new mode of communication with God; it was like an information download! He just placed an understanding in my head for something I had previously known *nothing* about.

We hadn't named Zachariah; his foster family did—but I *thought* we had named Esther—but apparently *not!* So now we needed to find our next daughter, Olive.

God was calling us to be a large family that would lead a *zoe* life. As a young Christian, I didn't know if this lined up with scripture, but I knew what He said. I called a Bible study friend, a more mature Christian, and inquired about the word *zoe*. She proceeded to tell me that *zoe* was the Aramaic word for "life." Jesus used that particular word when He said (translated to English):

---

*Name has been changed for privacy.

"The thief comes only to steal and kill and destroy. I came that they may have life and have it abundantly."

(John 10:10)

I then shared with her why I had asked, and she was overjoyed about the revelation God had given. She let me borrow some teaching tapes and books on the subject. I voraciously dove into the material.

Immediately, I began to learn all about *zoe*. This word for "life" has the connotation of being abundant and full, like our family. I even ordered a new license plate for the family van that said "PRO ZOE." I had thought Esther was the pinnacle of our calling, but God had a much bigger plan than I could conceive of in my human finitude and Christian infancy.

At the time, I didn't realize the magnitude of the need behind this calling from God. I later found out, though Blacks comprise just 13% of US population, 38% of all abortions are Black children. To meet the demand, or to fuel it, Planned Parenthood placed 78% of their clinics in high Black population areas—a terrible formula for disaster relative to the future of this race.

Dave and I started to pray and fast on a regular basis because we had learned this particular Christian discipline can help bring spiritual breakthroughs. We had another daughter out there, somewhere, but *how* were we to find her?! You can't call an agency and ask if they have any Olives on their books. We knew God was going to have to give us very specific directives or deliver Olive to the front door. Months passed; we continued to fast regularly and pray for knowledge to help find our little girl. We hoped to receive insight from the adoption realm.

The world of adoption is a small place, and you get to know many of the people in it. But in the 1990s, people who were involved in transracial, special needs adoption weren't just a small group—it was minuscule. You got to know everyone. I was in a playgroup with a few other adoptive families who were similar to ours in diversity, quantity, and configuration. They were very few and far between, but some had transracial adoptions, others had children with birth disabilities like missing limbs, while some others, like ours, had both transracial and special needs kids.

One family was quite unique with 10 children, five biological and five medically critical special care adoptions. Their kids were profoundly disabled with issues like spina bifida, thrombocytopenia-absent radius (TAR) syndrome (similar to thalidomide babies), and even children who survived botched abortions. The mom, Cindy,* was trained as a registered nurse but was only plying her trade at home—nebulizers ran, medication schedules were adhered to, wheelchairs rolled around, a specially equipped car was in their driveway, the whole kit and caboodle.

Now, recall that I mentioned church service meetings were held at our house on Sunday nights? The body of believers was in our living room praying one of those evenings, and the phone rang. My initial thought was to let the machine get it, but then it occurred to me perhaps someone had gotten lost or couldn't find our house. As it jangled in its cradle, I tiptoed from the room in an effort to not be disruptive and quietly answered the phone in the kitchen, "Hello?" But it wasn't a lost soul; rather it was my friend Cindy from our adoption playgroup.

She and her husband were in the transition process with a little boy, Ethan*, who had cystic fibrosis. One of their special needs children had lived as long as his disabled body allowed and had gone to be with the Lord in heaven. Being selfless and giving, they chose to make room

---

*Name has been changed for privacy.

for another child in their big hearts and family. Ethan was in a foster home about 75 miles away. It was a lot of trouble because, with transition, you have to go back and forth multiple times, even in a single day, over a long period of time. But they were staunchly committed to adopting this little boy.

Cindy said she was having a problem with the foster home, and it was troubling her greatly. She needed to talk about it with someone who'd understand because she felt she must *do* something. She began to describe to me a little girl in the foster home and the troubling situation the foster family created by being painfully overt about not wanting her any longer. They made jokes to Cindy about a "two-for-one sale" right in front of the little one. She was three years old and had special needs, but for whatever reason, the foster mom wanted her home to be just for special needs *babies;* the little girl sadly wore out her welcome by the tender age of three.

It tore at my mother's heart that this family could have a child for so long, three years, and not develop any emotional bond. Cindy wanted to know if we knew anyone with an up-to-date home study who could potentially open up their home right away to help this little girl. By this point in the conversation, I'd started to get a warm feeling of resolve from the Holy Spirit as my heart went out to this unwanted child. So, I inquired, "Cindy, what is her name?"

She casually replied, "Olive, and she is just a darling little thing but has some pretty profound special needs." Of course, after hearing Olive's name, Cindy's voice faded away, and my heart was suffused with love for my little girl and excitement for what God was doing. I knew where she was now! I told Cindy unequivocally "Yes, I know a family—us."

Just like Joy with the dream about Esther, she proceeded to try to talk me out of it, saying we had too much on our plate, but I assured her I would call her the next day and tell her the whole story of why I was so sure. Cindy could have gone on to tell me she had two purple heads and four green feet, and I would have said "We can handle that!" But for now, I asked her to give me the caseworker's name and number at Children's Services.

Olive! The God of details continued to unfold His hand about our family's calling to a *zoe* life.

I returned to the church meeting so excited and waited for prayer to end before sharing the content of my conversation. Everyone was ecstatic. God was moving boldly on behalf of the calling He'd placed on our family. Going forward, Olive was going to be the object of many church members' ardent prayers.

The next day, I called the social worker downtown at Children's Services and was quite surprised when I was summarily stiff-armed with suspicion. I thought our willingness to adopt a difficult-to-place child like Olive would be well received. "What is going on?!" I thought to myself. I explained our family already had children of color in it, to allay that particular concern, and though I was not privy to her specific case, that we were willing and able to work with various special needs. She went on to explain the county had put together a long-term foster plan for Olive because her needs were too profound, and they didn't think a permanent placement was appropriate. She thanked me for my interest and quickly hung up.

Long-term foster care?!

NO!

Every child deserves a real forever home if at all possible!

I was not to be put off easily when I had a vocation from God. Though this is not typical with my rule-following, respect-for-authority nature, I went over her head and made another call to the case manager's boss.

The woman in charge of the unit was also wary of our intent, but I asked her why they made a long-term foster plan if a family was willing to adopt.

We continued to argue back and forth with the county over the next few weeks, and then Dave reached out to the office of the head of children's services (the *boss* of the boss of the boss of the caseworker). It is so hard to get in to see people in those lofty positions, so he finally wrote a letter. The letter was read by the chief of staff, and *she* got us in to see the head honcho. We explained our family scenario, our ability and willingness to handle Olive's issues, as well as our experience in the child welfare system. Ultimately, she agreed to look into our case with the social workers.

To demonstrate our readiness to do it their way, Dave and I signed up to become county foster parents and took countless hours of instruction and training. Not to blow our own horns, but we endured many classes we could have taught better than the inexperienced young social workers in charge. But we just needed the credit for instruction hours, so we had the kids cared for at home and tagged lengthy, boring classes onto the end of already long workdays.

We became certified foster parents and refused to drop the Olive case. Professionally, it looked irresponsible that they were just forging ahead with a long-term foster plan that was detrimental to child development. So finally, because of our months of persistence, they were forced to have a large-scale conference of all staff involved in Olive's custody case to make a permanent placement for her.

And they picked a different family—not us.

We were blown away.

Dumbfounded.

We could not *believe* it!

They explained the staff felt our large household was too busy for her to get the attention she needed, but they thanked us for our interest. This terrible disappointment occurred about seven months following my initial contact with the county. We had done all they'd asked of us—jumped through every hoop we could, like trick pony parents. So, I took the whole situation to the only One who knows what happened in the hearts and minds of the Children's Services staff, my heavenly Father.

I poured out my heart to Him in tears and petition. I tried to leave it in His hands, but I was grieving for my daughter. I knew that she was our daughter. Grief snuck up on me regularly; the painful catch in my throat stole my breath, and the tears just flowed and flowed. One day, as the kids were having their nap, I was out mowing the lawn, and the roaring engine was obnoxiously loud, but I shouted into the air, "Satan, you are in such big trouble because my Father hates it when you make me cry!"

It is quite natural when things go awry to question yourself—what you did or didn't do—and I went down that second-guessing road:

Did I push too hard with Children's Services?

Did I miss God?

Was it actually what He said?

Could there be a different Olive somewhere?!

I thought through and prayed about it all and came up totally empty.

I just knew Children's Services had some issue with us and had looked for any reason they could find to deny us custody. Then, I reminded myself of who is truly in charge—God doesn't just try, He finishes what He begins:

"And I am sure of this, that he who began a good work in you will bring it to completion at the day of Jesus Christ."

(Philippians 1:6)

"But it still hurts." I wept to God, crying for a daughter I had yet to meet but held close in my heart. I came upon a scripture in Luke that says Jesus will have His day:

"But first He must suffer many things and be rejected by this generation."

(Luke 17:25)

I felt as though the Lord was telling me the same, and I was to deal with the bitter rejection, allowing it to mature me in my faith. I wouldn't allow this puzzling turn of events to distract me from my purpose, discourage me in my faith, or get me to be offended and off God's calling. Rejection was a sign to Luke that he was in the center of God's will—so it's a good sign for me too, even if it feels terrible.

A few weeks passed, I was still standing on God's promise of Olive and trusting in His sovereignty. My prayer had been that God would give us favor even as the devil was doing his best to make the social workers suspicious of us.

"For you bless the righteous, O Lord; you cover him with favor as with a shield."

(Psalm 5:12)

The end of October was approaching, and the phone jangled in its cradle again, but this time in the middle of the day. Oddly, it was Olive's social worker, whose voice I'd come to know and not particularly care for.

"We were wondering if you and your husband might still be interested in parenting Olive?" she inquired sheepishly.

I had to ask her to repeat herself.

It was so hard to understand her.

She must have been eating crow at the time.

My heart was doing somersaults, and blood was rushing in my ears!

"WHAT?!—Of course! Why? What happened? Actually, forget it—I don't *care* what happened."

I blurted out, "Yes, we'd love to!" But the social worker told me I couldn't just accept on the phone and that we had to come downtown, read her complete file, sign off on a paper, and give our consent that we knew what was involved relative to the special needs noted in Olive's case file.

Apparently, the people the county had chosen as "best" to parent Olive never even bothered to meet her. They read her file and were completely put off by the special needs she currently displayed and those that may develop in the future due to her birth circumstances. They just didn't want to go forward with the county's plan despite being their chosen ones as her parents.

So, on Satan's high holy day, Halloween, Dave and I got ready and went downtown to Children's Services to defy the enemy of our souls and read Olive's file in its entirety. Her life began with great difficulty as she was addicted to crack and had syphilis at birth, which unfortunately went untreated. Also, we had no idea how it might manifest in her life later on, but we had faith in God and His plan for her life, including us as her parents. So, we signed the papers to begin the process of transitioning our daughter to her rightful God-given place in this world—in our family.

I'll never forget the first Sunday I held her in church, her downy hair against my cheek and her happy little self, relaxed in my lap. God is incredible. He can do so much more than we could ever ask or think.

(Ephesians 3:20)

The transition was taxing on all of us as I put over 2,000 miles on the family van in just two months! And Olive was rightfully confused about why she had to leave her foster family. She was not privy to the foster parent's opinions, but we handled her feelings and tantrums as best we could, with prayer and patience.

Olive's deliverance from "the system" was a miracle, but she would also prove to be quite an addition to our expanding household and our adventure in God, requiring me to grow and mature in ways I'd never thought possible or necessary.

Six kids: Zachariah, Olive, Ester (front row) Daniel, Sarah, Nathan (back row).

Trisha Tangent:

Trisha's Tantrum Technique

Tantrums can be so difficult, rough on parent and child alike, strenuous, awkward, humiliating, or emotional. I've lived through quite a few, and Olive had many during her transition. I have learned several things that can reduce the duration, frequency, and pain.

First, I prayed. Regardless of whether it is at home or in public, the child is out of control, and the enemy loves that particular playground. I prayed for protection, evenness in the child's emotions, and for resolution.

Next, when a tantrum occurred, I made sure the child knew I saw it but I was not attending to it. It is an unacceptable way to express yourself or to "get your way," and children need to learn tantrums *don't work*. Some experts say to ignore them completely, but my experience says you need to go one step further. Acknowledge its existence and then act like you won't pay any attention to it.

In my experience, the child usually threw themselves on the floor or ground. At this point, I had them right where I wanted them. I'd make a huge, overly dramatic step *across* the child and then just walk away. I literally walked over them, so obviously I saw the display, and they knew I did. If I was in a store, I just stayed in the aisle ahead of them, perusing the merchandise and using my peripheral vision to keep an eye on them.

If they ramped up, I turned my back completely, or if I was in a small local store where I felt comfortable, I would turn the corner. (**Do not** do this if you are in a big-box store or someplace unfamiliar because there are just too many dangerous, predatory people around!) When kids realize you won't attend to this foolishness, they typically gear down and stop.

After the hyperventilating was over and the nose stopped running, I'd sit down and talk about it. I never attempted to do this when they were still emotionally ramped up because it would start all over again. I told them in simple, but no uncertain terms, that I would not address their issues when they throw a fit. Ever.

If it is a "gimme" problem in a store, it similarly *never* worked. I did not give in, even when they *did* calm down because that would become the norm. They'd throw the fit and then calm down in order to get the toy or candy or whatever. I *never* let it work. I'd tell them what would happen if the tantrum happened again, and I'd follow through to the letter.

Once, I was in a small local hardware store, and they had lollipops displayed for sale on the counter. When the I-want-a-lollipop tantrum started, I turned on my heel, winked at the employee (whom I knew) at the register, left the merchandise, *stepped over the fit-throwing child,* and headed for the door. Earlier, when all was calm and we were heading to the store, I told the preschooler I was going to leave if we had any behavioral issues, and I did just what I said.

Eventually, the tantrums stop altogether because we *never* let them work, but I did go through the anti-tantrum process with several of our kids.

SideNote:

If a special needs child has a "sensory meltdown", when one or more of their five senses are overstimulated and giving them anxiety or distress of some kind, it is NOT a temper tantrum. Psychosomatic attention-seeking "illness" can often be remedied by ignoring it, just like attention-seeking manipulative tantrums. Depriving a tantrum of attention, and not allowing it to "work" on you, can often stop the behavior.

But this tantrum technique won't be helpful with a sensory meltdown.

As a parent, you will learn to discern the difference. Some kids need the stimulation removed such as going into a quiet darkened room or just applying noise canceling headphones to their ears. When I felt an overreaction from a child was sensory overload, my children typically needed deep sensory input instead of elimination.

If we were at home, we would make a pillow "sandwich" with two large floor pillows. One pillow on the floor, the child on top and the second pillow on top of them with my weight added for deeper compression, if necessary. My autistic son always loved a "Sean Sandwich" when he needed it. If a meltdown occurred in public, sometimes a healthy bear hug could give enough sensory input to get us safely home.

Train up a child in the way he should go;
even when he is old he will not depart from it.

(Proverbs 22:6)

4

Procedures in Parenting

Though it was a daily battle, we refused to allow chaos to triumph in our household. As maturing young Christians, Dave and I pressed into God for the growing needs of this big, beautiful family. We were desperate for His direction to help us in this sizable parenting adventure since neither of us were from very large families.

Innumerable tasks had to be tackled daily, and He graciously provided creative ideas for us to keep our lives organized, disciplined, and flowing smoothly. We had so many activities, appointments, school assignments, practices, and therapies; we really needed Him to help us get our parenting act together.

Thankfully, the "big" kids, ages six, eight, and 10, began to understand the saying I had posted on the refrigerator:

"The more we do *together*, the more we can *do* together!"

Dave and I only had two hands each—we could *not* be all things to all people in our home! We had tried a myriad of organizational styles with different job charts, chore wheels with stickers, and the like, but they always seemed to be corrupted by kids (stolen, moved, or *eaten* stickers), or the system just fell by the wayside because it wasn't user friendly.

Prior to motherhood, when I first got out of college and was newly married, I was a teacher (middle school and high school social studies) and a coach (three seasons: field hockey, basketball, and track). Teaching and coaching were my early training grounds to prepare me as a mother of many! Oftentimes, I needed to be innovative with organization and discipline in my classes and on my teams, so I was super frustrated by our household bedlam; a solution had to be found. What we *greatly* needed was a system the kids themselves were committed to, not just their parents! That was what worked best in the long run with both my students and players—*they* needed to take responsibility and be the impetus for any system to work.

God provided inspiration for this ever-increasing need when we developed what we called "the peg system." It came together after a lot of trial and error, reading, and talking with other moms, but I truly believed in the system. In all its fullness, it was a God-originated idea. This chore and reward system worked for years, and it made a big difference in our day-to-day home life.

We had some simple foundational ground rules for Dave and me:

Parent Rule #1

We had to teach our children to do the chores if we wanted them done well. We didn't expect them to learn just by having watched us do it a million times. Trust me, we knew they were *not* paying attention, so they couldn't replicate our efforts.

Parent Rule #2

We had to be mindful of age and size. Responsibilities had to be commensurate with their comprehension and ability. We got some it's-not-fair grousing at the outset, but we turned it right back on them because it certainly was not fair for things to go on with only adults shouldering all responsibility. There were plenty of chores within the realm of the children's capabilities.

Parent Rule #3

Dave and I had a motto: "Children don't do what you *ex*-pect, they do what you *in*-spect." We were prepared to be overly vigilant at the outset and tapered off as we built trust in their ability to follow through and to be consistent and thorough.

"The Peg System"

I had my talented woodworker father make a pegboard for each child with their names proudly displayed in the middle with an engraved brass plaque. Four pegs hung on each board from little pieces of rawhide inset by four bored holes. No pieces could disappear. Each peg was to be placed in its respective hole on a daily basis as the kids accomplished their responsibilities associated with each color: yellow, red, green, and blue.

The yellow peg was the "morning peg"—yellow like the sunrise. Before the morning peg went in the hole, they had to make their bed, brush their teeth, and be dressed and ready for school *on time*. Once they completed these tasks, then the yellow peg could go into its hole. The kids even seemed to derive some satisfaction from placing the peg into its hole with a *thunk*, but that wasn't the only inspiration.

The red peg was the "chore peg" and was done after school. It's red because they had to stop their current activity to do the peg. Each child had a room to straighten (just pick up and straighten), a job to do (like sweep the stairs or empty the hamper), and one task to help with dinner (like empty the dishwasher, set the table, help the cook, or clear the table). After their jobs were done, the red peg would go into its hole.

The green peg was the "growth peg" and was also done after school. It involved all the things that make children grow into good people, thus green for growth. We presented a scripture each week, and they were to work on memorization to recite it on Saturday. Each child was to do their homework and practice whatever extracurricular they were currently learning, e.g., piano or dance. Green also meant they could *go*. Once the green peg was in, they could ask to *go* to a friend's house, ask to *go* watch a video (this was the '90s!), or ask to *go* play outside.

Finally, the blue peg was the nighttime peg. They had to brush their teeth, say their prayers, and be in bed *on time* to earn their blue peg. When they were little, they also had to make their "clothes person" on the floor in their rooms. Each piece of clothing was laid out for the next day so it was all ready to put on, and it helped a great deal to move the morning routine along. Plus, they liked laying it out to look like a person on the carpet, whether it was school uniform or church clothes.

Just before bedtime, each child would bring a small slip of paper to Mom or Dad with the number of pegs achieved that day, and we would sign it as being accurate. The little "chits" went into a box, and at the end of the week, it was opened up, and all the signed chits were tallied. No unsigned chits counted, or we would have had an early lesson in ballot-box stuffing. Efforts to get around our checks were met with consequences, financial and otherwise.

This then introduces the economic side of the peg system. Payday.

We wanted our children to understand a bit of the economic side of life and how to be a good steward of what God provides. We felt the peg system planted seeds of fiscal responsibility in their hearts because it invested in their education of how the financial world works, both where the money comes from (money is earned) *and* how to use it responsibly (save, give, or spend).

Campbell Core Values

(Prominently posted in the kitchen)

*Love God

*Family First (after God)

*Work Hard

*Tell the Truth

*Be Kind

*Manners Matter

Since kids often need more money when they are older, we paid relative to their age (we paid a nickel per year of age. So if you were five, you got a quarter for each peg, at 10 you got $.50 per peg, and so on) and then by the number of pegs earned. Additionally, because we wanted to reward the character qualities of being faithful, consistent, and diligent, when a child got all four pegs *every* day, they were paid *double*. On payday, they recited the Bible memory verse of the week. (It varied by age—the younger ones had a small chunk whereas the big kids had a full verse) Then, they were "paid" relative to the number of pegs they achieved.

Since we were trying to convey the idea of how the world works, they didn't receive the whole lump, but rather they were to decide, like in adult life, how much to save, invest, and give. They had to save at least 10%, "invest" (it went toward some longer-term goal that varied per child), and give at least 10% to the church, just as they tithed in the Bible. Dave kept track in the "Bank of Campbell" on his computer.

They got to choose how they wanted to handle the balance. If a friend's birthday party was coming up, they may need to put it in savings so they could buy their friend a gift. Or, they may want to take savings out because they outgrew their bicycle or had finished saving up for something they wanted.

What we were actually doing is giving money to our children so they could learn good life lessons while getting chores done around the house. We felt it was far better than "allowance," which is handed out freely, because peg money is tied to how well you worked, just like in life. Everyone had an economic incentive to pitch in for our family, and it also gave them a little bit of financial power over their own lives. They could also do additional chores to earn extra money if they wanted to save up faster for something they wanted or needed. Just like real life, when you want something you have to work for it.

Because of this system, each child felt they had a bit of financial authority over how their life flowed. Prior to the peg system, they only had money from birthdays or Christmas. Because they had some discretionary money each week, it gave them a modicum of power over their lives and allowed them to have some control over things they wanted to have, places they wanted to go, or things they wanted to do.

You want to go to the movies with friends? Sure, if you have enough in your account.

You want the latest, greatest video game? Sure, if you have enough in your account (and the game shouldn't be violent).

You want a candy bar in the checkout line at the grocery? Sure, if you have enough in your account.

I rarely had to deal with the "gimmes" at the grocery store because the answer was always the same—as long as you have enough money in your account."

Similarly, I didn't feel like I had to nag about things because I could just ask if their pegs were done. One afternoon, our oldest son, Daniel, came home from school, saw the green light on the dishwasher, and yelled, "I call it!" He wanted to accomplish his "help with dinner" responsibility because he wanted to get his red and green pegs done since he had friends to play with and places to go. He was only 10 years old, and he came home from school in search of what he could do to help with dinner! Genuinely seeking a way to pitch in!

He knew I would ask if his pegs were done, so he just *did them.* When he asked to go play with his friends and I inquired if his pegs were done, he answered honestly that they were done. And having developed trust in his adherence to the system, I didn't have to nag about what was or wasn't done. I could just say, "Have fun and stay safe." Yes! Thank you, Lord—this is how I had hoped it would work! I was so very grateful.

The peg system served our family well for many years and was another example of God's creativity in providing for our need; it gave us a way to organize our large household, teach the kids responsibility with chores and money, and provide some help and peace (Amen!) for the adults.

We always took weekends off from the peg system so it never became onerous, and they were more willing to stick with it. Similarly, we had seasons of illness or times of vacation, and the pegs fell by the wayside. But the kids *wanted* to get back to it for financial reasons, and the adults *wanted* to return to the pegs for structure, so we commenced the system once life settled back to normal. It was our hope the peg system would create a lifelong habit to put responsibilities before privileges because we wanted them to have self-discipline that would serve them well into adulthood.

Trisha Tangent:

Training, Teaching, Coaching

Children need guidance and rules, but they vary a lot by age, child, and personality. Here are a few concepts we found to work.

When we dealt with preschoolers, we knew it was time to **train**. We used small, short sentence segments for the rules and trained them to be the kind of children we sought to raise. Our preschool rules were simple and to the point:

1. "Listen and do." You have to start young if you want your children to submit to authority (teachers, coaches, pastors, bosses, etc.) and it starts with you. When I asked them to do something, and they were not receptive, I'd say "Listen and do" which indicated they were potentially breaking that rule.

2. "Inside voice": The decibel level in a family with this many children could be deafening. They had to learn to use their inside voice—especially in the close confines of the car!

3. "Walking feet": Little ones at every turn and lots of hurried feet is a formula for accidents—they had to walk indoors.

4. "Body to self": This rule incorporated all parts of the body, so the rule was particularly helpful with boys who could be ingenious at encroachment on a sister's space without using their actual hands.

5. "Be kind": Simple and straightforward. This covers many potential aggressions.

6. "Tell the truth": Again, simple and straightforward. They know truth from lies.

Six simple rules. Not long or verbose.

When they got to school age, we advanced to **teaching**. Some were ready by four, but most started this phase at elementary school age.

We taught in five parts; the last one was independence:

1. "Watch me": Whatever you are trying to teach, cooking, sewing, any chores, construction, etc., the very first level is — Watch me do it.

2. "Help me": In this phase, the child is your assistant, and you can even go so far as putting their hands on your hands and let them assist—Help me do it.

3. "I help you": In this phase, the child is now doing the activity you are teaching, and you are *their* assistant. You are just there to correct and guide them hands-on—I help you.

4. "Watch you": Now it is your turn to watch and make sure no harm comes to the child and give verbal prompts if you see things coming off the rails—I watch you.

5. Independence: Now they should be able and trustworthy to handle the job by themselves!

(A special note about my trouble with perfection. I *had* to be delivered from perfectionism because "fixing" or "adjusting" after my child accomplished any chore was *not* an option. Nothing undermines a child's confidence and self-worth like a parent entrusting a job to them and then redoing it when they are done! Especially if you praise them, then they find you later on trying to make it perfect—smoothing out the wrinkles in their efforts. It's just like saying, "I need help," and then after they help, you say, "Not like that! Forget it—I'll do it.")

We trained and taught early on, but when we reached high school age, it was time to **coach**. Teens don't want to be talked down to like they are being trained, nor do they believe they need to be taught any longer. Teens prefer to be coached through mistakes and encouraged through difficulties. The car was a great place for coaching because it didn't involve eye contact, which tended to make it more intense for them. We also had a captive audience while driving, so we could complete our sentences!

For instance, one of the boys was having difficulty with bullies at school and did *not* want us to intervene as he was in an all-boys high school. He didn't want to appear to have his parents fight his battles. We were able to give guidance and direction about handling the situation when the most nettlesome bully had a serious and rather embarrassing sports injury. He could no longer play hockey and many of the other players had abandoned him since they were uncomfortable with his injury. It was a bit of a social minefield because "popular" kids were involved, but we coached Daniel through it, and he was a better friend and greater light for the Gospel because of it.

We asked Dan how he would feel in that boy's situation. (As a good lifelong habit, it's always good to get kids to consider walking in someone else's shoes.)

How would he want to be treated?

How were the other teammates treating the injured player? (They all avoided him.)

What could you do differently?

When coaching a teen, it's all about encouraging them to analyze and assess a situation; think it through and then act accordingly. Every player I ever coached was better off in game situations when they had thought through and practiced various scenarios *prior* to the game. That is exactly what we were trying to get our kids to do, to *respond* to life events, not *react*.

In this situation, Daniel decided to just visit the boy, as it seemed to be the friendliest thing he could do. The other boys were embarrassed by the injury and were antisocial toward him. As I recall, he brought him some sports magazines and talked to him about *anything* but his injury. Daniel definitely showed himself to be guided by the light of the Gospel rather than the whims of teen social hierarchy. The boy's mother was so very thankful for Dan's visit and told us how much she appreciated his kind gesture.

Our son was blessed by our coaching through that difficult time, but I'd say all our teens felt more encouraged and mentored when we used a coach-like parenting style. Additionally, if we needed to impart knowledge, we did so with a certain amount of diffidence to make our teen feel as though they were remembering something they already knew but had forgotten. Particularly, we did this with scriptural things, where we sort of reminded them to make them aware of it even though it may slip their mind. They were far more receptive to our input when it felt less like parental directives and more like guidance in helping them respond to difficult and often thorny teen issues.

Another way God helped us get our parental act together, in addition to the peg system, was by inspiring us with strategies for discipline. Dave and I learned quickly that if we were systematic about it and united on discipline, it would help the kids to know what was expected.

It was also good at making *them* mind without losing *our* minds!

The spade of discipline worked best when it dug deep to the root of the child's issue. We found three types of consequences that worked well, especially when used in order.

1. Natural: if at all possible, we let the natural consequences rain down hard. We found that with particularly strong-willed kids, we had to augment with additional discipline. But most often, the natural consequences taught the best. For example, I didn't give out punishment when they left toys around. They got cleaned up when I vacuumed, but to get them back, they had to do a chore. The lesson I wanted them to learn was that things can disappear if you don't take care of them, even in adulthood.

2. Logical: if no natural consequences existed or *we* needed to add to the direction-giving load to drive home a point, we used logical consequences, something that made sense with the infraction. For instance, if a child lied about doing their homework and the natural consequence came down at school for not doing it, we also disciplined them at home for lying. We made them copy it over twice—do the homework and then rewrite it as their consequence for the lie. It was a good way to drive home a learning concept *and* give them a logical consequence. The classic logical one they all dreaded was if they missed the school bus—they had to walk to school, and

I walked with them. It was no small consequence when we had moved back to the suburbs because the high school was a little over four miles away, the middle school was four and a half, and the elementary a little further than that! We often had people stop along the way to try to give us a ride, and I'd nonchalantly respond, "Thank you! No, we don't need a ride. Family discipline." The kids thought I was daft when we were three miles into it, but they *rarely* missed the bus after the experience of that particular logical consequence.

3. Artificial: if no natural or logical consequences were able to drive home a lesson, then we had to use artificial consequences. This included time-outs, grounding, early bedtime, and the like. (Though such things can be "logical" as well for infractions involving curfew or messing around at bedtime, etc.)

   (Note on the artificial use of time-outs: When they were young, I never gave more than one minute per year of age. If I went much longer, they didn't even remember the connection to their infraction. Additionally, when an argument or fight broke out, *both* kids got the time-out. After the least number of minutes per the youngest child, I went to the time-out bench and each one had to say what *they* did wrong in the situation. Even if it was just for being argumentative or disagreeing between themselves, if they started to blame-shift and say "well, *they* were ...," the time-out started all over again. We were the judge and jury on what were to be any further consequences. After all, our family was not a democracy, but what we liked to call a "benign dictatorship." Mom and Dad were in charge but with everyone's best interests in mind. Period. Though this may sound harsh to a democratic American mind, this approach gives an incredible amount of security to a child.)

These guidelines were helpful in determining consequences for infractions of various family rules, disobedience, willfulness, and the like. The kids rarely protested it to be unfair when the consequence was logical to the infraction. But like I said, sometimes we had to use them *all*, but we did so in order.

When you dig deep near the root of the problem, you help them to grow through discipline rather than feel like they are being punished.

A good example of the discipline types used in order occurred when Olive was in second grade and we were still living in Cleveland. She told a whopper of a lie at school, bragging that she was related to Jane Campbell, who was then the mayor of Cleveland, Ohio.

I received a distressed call from her teacher at her special needs school after the class had been in an uproar for two days due to this braggadocious child. With trepidation, the teacher/nun asked if we were related to Jane Campbell so she could settle the matter in her classroom of upset seven-year-olds, several of whom had mood disorders. I told her we absolutely were *not related*! But *now* I understood why Olive worked herself into a fever that same morning and stayed home "sick"; she was avoiding her self-made classroom chaos!

I had a frank conversation with her about honesty and being a good friend, making it clear to her that she needed to go to school the next day and make things right with her friends (natural consequence) by telling the truth. (PS—I would have taken her to school when I figured out the lie, but it was late in the day and her school was 15 miles away.)

The next day, the teacher called me back because the truth had not been told; in fact, the story had ramped up even further. It was quite unbelievable! Now, not only was the honorable Jane Campbell supposed to be her aunt, but she had been promoted to Olive's own personal godmother! She probably would have tried to label her "fairy godmother" if she thought she could have pulled it off!

Okay, I reasoned to myself, this needed direct parental intervention, in person. Immediately, I hopped in the van and headed straight to her school.

As I drove to the school, I endured a 15-mile drive of self-recriminations on my fitness as a mother. I tried to call Dave for some spousal support, but he was in meetings. Darn it. I arrived, barely surviving my own accusatory where-did-I-go-wrong?! barrage. I prayed in the parking lot, got myself settled, and was ready with a plan to usher her through this debacle with our disciplinary strategy: natural, logical, then artificial consequences.

Entering the school, the secretary looked up for a second, but she appeared to know I was expected and waved me past. Oh dear, everyone else I passed in the hallway appeared to be anticipating my arrival. This really was disruptive! I arrived at the second-grade classroom, and I sheepishly knocked on the door, not wanting to interrupt.

The flustered nun, who had obviously had a difficult morning, saw my face in the little peek-a-boo door window and waved at me to come in, as if she was saying, "Come! Come! Come—get in here now!" She wanted this whole thing straightened out, pronto! Having grown up Catholic, I was full of dread, butterflies in my chest as if I myself was the child in trouble with this nun!

Taking my daughter by the hand, I walked her from her desk to a private corner and sat down on a child's chair, looking like a spindly-legged giant as the knees to my towering 5' 11" self rose to meet my chest. As I sat across from Olive, I put my hands on hers and gave her direct eye contact. With my serious I-mean-business mom-face affixed and a low-volume, patient voice, I explained that her story was out of hand and got in the way of classroom instruction by disrupting the other children. The truth needed to be told.

I told her to go to the front of the class and set the record straight (an embarrassing but logical consequence). I encouraged her by quoting the scripture, "You can do all things through Christ who strengthens you" (Philippians 4:13 New King James Version, a recent peg system scripture memory verse from home). I explained again how disruptive and upsetting it was to her classmates, but she would *not* tell the truth.

Frustrated, but not letting it show on my face, I pulled out the "big guns," a hard-hitting artificial consequence. I threatened her with her upcoming birthday party. "If you don't set this straight, it just shows me you don't care much about your classmates, and we will have to cancel your birthday party with your school friends later this month" (artificial, though I tried to make it somewhat logical).

She dug in her heels, folded her little arms across her chest, her eyes narrowed, then she refused to comply with an emphatic, pouty "no" that had a bit of an underlying snarl. She wouldn't budge.

Releasing a long-held sigh, I arose from my teeny tiny chair and said, "Fine, it has to be done, and if you won't tell your friends the truth, then I will." I strode to the front of the class and told them our family was in no way related to Jane Campbell, and I was so sorry the story had disrupted their classroom learning.

A little girl's hand shot into the air. Unprepared to take questions, I pointed at the little one and said, "Yes, honey?"

"Who's Jane Campbell?" she asked.

Smack my head.

Our family celebrated Olive's birthday later that month, but the friend party did not take place. We never threatened any consequence if we were not prepared to follow through. The child's loss of parental respect and security wouldn't be worth it.

True to His Word, God consistently gave us inspiration when we needed help in this over-the-top parenting adventure. By His grace, He kept us organized and disciplined in creative and effective ways, hoping to create good lifelong habits to bless our kids, their spouses, and their own children as well. And we *needed* to be organized because He was going to call us out on another adventure, but this time *with* the children.

Amusing Anecdote

Our daughters, Olive and Esther, were in ballet class together because they were so close in age. Olive took it very seriously, and Esther just liked the tutu and was amused and silly. They had a little recital for the families, and our less serious ballerina, Esther, being silly and theatrical, proceeded to toot (flatulate) every time the girls had a plié! It was all I could do to keep my other kids (and our nanny, Michelle!) from completely losing it! It was pretty funny, and on a couple of them, she looked right at us, crossed her eyes, gave a huge grin, did her plié and—toot!

... Truly I understand that God shows no partiality,
but in every nation anyone who fears Him and does
what is right is acceptable to Him.

(Acts 10:34–35)

5

All Aboard for Babylon

We needed more diversity. Inside our house was fine, because we had everything, from porcelain to café au lait to chocolate faces, a rich variety of life experiences, plus lots of interactions with various body types, hair, and skincare—but outside our house fell short of the proverbial diversity mark.

Our children had a wonderful, racially varied family and were comfortable in a wide range of settings from the inner-city projects to the country club but needed the world around them to reflect that same receptivity of differences. Our new young church had a few families of color, but the town we lived in was very heavily Caucasian, and though we were never overtly rejected, it sometimes felt like we were accepted as a novelty act. At times, we were definitely the sole source of diversity for others because we were surrounded by Whiteness in our neighborhood. We needed to find other avenues of diverse interaction for ourselves. Our all-knowing God was about to call us out on an adventure for that very purpose.

We didn't want the kids to feel "different." We tried to be transparent with them that God had made our family in a different way and, though we may not be typical, we were totally "normal." We had our adoption playgroup with families just like ours, which was quite helpful, but in the end, God gave us a bold call to move from the suburbs to the city where diversity was at every turn.

"For you will spread abroad to the right and to the left, and your offspring will possess the nations and will people the desolate cities."

(Isaiah 54:3 ESV)

God wanted us to leave our newly expanded suburban home to go into the city of Cleveland and be a light. This adventure was going to involve a whole lot of unsettling change for our kids who often need more stability than most. But we were up for the challenge and in it together. So, the search for our next home commenced.

During this season of time, my father, back in New England, had reached a critical stage in his deterioration with heart disease. Though now retired, during his career as a police officer he had lifted a drowned victim and had a heart attack. The coronary weakened his heart, making him susceptible, and he developed cardiomyopathy, a life-threatening enlargement of the heart. The quality of his life continued to dwindle, and he became so compromised that walking *down* a set of stairs made him break out in sweat from head to toe. My dad didn't trust the doctors at the small remote hospital in Maine he referred to as "Clamflat General." So, he finally traveled to Ohio to be seen by cardiologists at the world-class Cleveland Clinic.

They performed a new experimental surgical procedure, but it didn't help alleviate my dad's problem. His heart just couldn't pick up its beat again after the surgery. They had to crack his chest a second time and install a left ventricular assist device (LVAD), which was to run his heart by battery until a transplant became available. Thus, he was in the hospital for months as he awaited a donor's heart. My mom and I spent a great deal of time going back and forth to the Cleveland hospital, and it was on one of those many trips that a fortuitous thing happened; I found our new home in the city.

My mother and I had decided to decompress from the intense hospital day in the ICU by a leisurely ride home on slower streets, instead of the highway. We meandered through well-established neighborhoods along the lake where enormous ancient trees overarched the streets, like intertwined fingers of hands in prayer. It was a beautiful peaceful area, and unlike much of the city, it was less urban. We had discovered beautiful Edgewater Park.

Across the street from Lake Erie was a stately big old mansion with a "For Sale By Owner" sign. On seeing that, I got the same excited, warm, Holy Spirit feeling I'd experienced in the past when I was in the center of God's will. Dave and I made an appointment and went to see the place while my mom watched the kids.

The house was simply ideal for our big family.

It had been built in the 1920s as a clandestine home-based speakeasy during the Prohibition era and had some pretty crazy features. What a sense of humor God has, to turn a place originally designed for law-lessness into a home for a family who belonged to Him!

The house had a walk-in vault in the basement, just like a bank. The booze was smuggled across the lake from Canada, up from Lake Erie, through the tunnel, and then into the house without being seen! The tunnel had been backfilled with cement and covered with a loose steel plate, but the primary hole was still there on the floor of the vault! Additionally, a standing pipe fire hose was *in the house* so they could deal with any emergencies themselves; they didn't have to call the fire department since it would have exposed their covert operation.

A little peek-a-boo hinged window was designed in the front door like the one in the Emerald City from *The Wizard of Oz*. We would open it and shout, "Who rang that bell?!" just like the doorman with Dorothy. Lastly, the house had a crazy electrical system installed that allowed you to flicker all the lights in the entire house from right by the front door, a warning signal if imminent law enforcement "trouble" arrived. Our professional electrician said it was quite ingenious, and he couldn't figure out how they had done it!

Other than those peculiarities, it was a big (over 7,500 square feet!), beautiful house with a ton of old-world character and charm, which really appealed to me as my mom was an antique dealer: inlaid walnut doors, some with leaded and stained glass windows, crystal and ceramic doorknobs, enormous plaster crown moldings, beautiful hand-wrought ironwork with flowers and trailing vines, and ten-foot ceilings, plus lots of modern updates to make life easier. We needed to transform the third floor's 2,000-square-foot oak-floored ballroom into more bedrooms and bathrooms for our ever-expanding brood, but that was an easy design fix for our wonderful architect who had created the plans for our previous suburban house addition.

A much-needed and enormous renovated kitchen was already done. Plus, there was a tremendous amount of entertainment space; the living room alone was 800 square feet, and the dining room was so big that we once had a sit-down dinner for 44 people—and it wasn't even crowded!

A feature the kids found to be fun for games of tag and hide-and-seek was the five staircases. When it was first built, the house was separated into two sides—one was for the owners and their guests, and the other was the servants' side. There was a palatial grand staircase on the owner's side and a serviceable back staircase on the one for the servants. So, there were two stairs to the basement, two stairs to the second floor, and one staircase up to the third-floor ballroom. A rambunctious kid's dream!

God also used our new home for a *lot* of our church's ministry throughout the years, but most of all, He brought our family into the city where diversity was the norm. And there was just so much grist for this diversity mill; Black, White, Middle Eastern, Hispanic, Slavic, rich, poor, straight, gay, political, apolitical, artistic, academic, you name it! One time, I had to explain to the kids why a tall Black man with a huge Afro was struggling to cross the street in high-heeled white patent leather boots, a tight midriff-baring shirt, and bright-pink hot pants; but it was typical, everyday life in the city! Our ongoing adventures with God were expansive and, now, much more diverse.

In our new city neighborhood, one of our next-door neighbors was a leading homosexual activist. He was very well connected—formerly a Cleveland Clinic doctor who had transitioned to a career as a high-end clothing and jewelry designer for many of Cleveland's elite. About a year after we had arrived in the area, Dave crossed paths with him on a stroll in the neighborhood. Just being his usual friendly and polite self, he asked the gentleman, who had lived there for decades, what was the biggest change he had seen in the Edgewater area over the years.

Trisha's Tangent:

Michelle Joins the Family

When God calls you to do something, He not only gives the vision but the *pro*vision. In our particular calling, we needed a lot of extra adult support. A number of times, He sent people to help who were with us for a short season of time to get on their feet or to get their own ministry off the ground. They lived with us, helped with our kids, and we gave them free room and board. The greatest of these childcare angels was Michelle; plus, she was *my* Timothy (Acts 16:1, 1 Cor. 4:17, 1 Thess. 3:2).

She came to live with us at the same time we were called to move into the city. For room and board, she helped with the kids, just as the others had done. But with Michelle, it was a bit different. God kept upping the ante with her, calling her to do more and be more. As our family grew and changed, our demands on her time expanded. But she didn't shrink from the call, rather she embraced it and took the childcare challenge as her own calling from God. And she was wonderful with kids!

As we move forward in the book, she will be included in our story when we were called to the city, and she became like a tag-team wrestler with me! You know what I mean, where one guy is wrestling and then he gets worn out and tags his teammate who then comes in to replace him and keep the wrestling going. That was us. I'd go one way with a bunch of kids; she went another. Or I'd stay and cook while she went on a pickup run. We were tag-team wrestling our family! Somehow, someway, we managed to get it all covered.

(Note: We had a rule that the kids could have one extracurricular activity each season. So, if you played basketball, you couldn't try out for the musical too! After all, for them, it was only one, but for us, it was *eight extracurriculars*—imagine if we allowed two each?!)

Michelle learned to cook and was willing to help clean. She picked up the laundry chore almost immediately since I often found her folding clothes, and she would say she kind of enjoyed it! Well, be my guest—please!

We had so many washers and dryers over the years, and we had one repairman who was blunt with us. He said, "Frankly, you are using a residential machine in a commercial fashion." He was right. Between the school uniform clothes, play clothes, sports clothes, and Sunday's church clothes, those machines ran for hours every single day. But Michelle got a great deal of satisfaction from laundry, as if she was sorting out life itself, one load at a time.

At one point, Michelle changed her job availability to part time and was paid to work part time for us. Then during a season when I got sick, we paid her to go full time for our family. She was always flexible, amenable, and willing to change in any way we needed.

Earlier I mentioned her as my "Timothy" who became the right-hand man to Paul in his ministry. Interestingly, Timothy had no father and was raised by his mother and grandmother. Michelle, similarly, had no father as he had died of a heart attack when she was only two weeks old. Michelle once told me that she had a pretty poor family life growing up and she felt blessed to be a part of healthy family interactions.

Ultimately, God made her one of the Campbell clan, and we wouldn't have it any other way. We bless each other. Her endless humor makes us laugh. We love her, and she loves us, which is God's design for this family. Everybody in this atypical household arrived in a different way, but the beauty is we all arrived, and God knit us together. Michelle is still with us to this very day.

In our new city neighborhood, one of our next-door neighbors was a leading homosexual activist. He was very well connected—formerly a Cleveland Clinic doctor who had transitioned to a career as a high-end clothing and jewelry designer for many of Cleveland's elite. About a year after we had arrived in the area, Dave crossed paths with him on a stroll in the neighborhood. Just being his usual friendly and polite self, he asked the gentleman, who had lived there for decades, what was the biggest change he had seen in the Edgewater area over the years.

He expected him to say something about the turnover of the local retail area or mansions being massively renovated, but Dave said he surprisingly didn't lose a beat and said, "You! Without a doubt, your family moving in was the biggest change that's happened *by far*!" He was very complimentary of our polite children, which does a mother's heart good, but I was thankful he had observed our lives and our demeanor as neighbors. I pray he someday will seek the One who made us so wonderfully different in his eyes, "a royal priesthood, a holy nation, a people for His own possession" (1 Peter 2:9) worthy of his notice.

Notably, the other neighbors included an Eastern European couple; the wife spoke several languages and taught them at college level. She loved our kids and blessed them often during the orthodox holidays. Across the street was a Ukrainian couple who renovated a lakeside mansion where President Franklin Delano Roosevelt once had lunch. They had an adopted daughter who played often with Olive and Esther. At the end of the block was a doctor and his wife who tore down the house next to them just to build a sculpture garden. The kids and I had great fun making up names for each successive sculpture she added— distinguished names included "Raptor Nail with Polish," "Flying Tackle," and "Giant Sequoia Hunk."

One quiet winter's day, I saw a neighborhood baby toddling down our side street in a diaper! I quickly ran out to grab him before a car could come along, but thankfully, our street was quiet. Wrapping him in my knit vest, as I hadn't taken time to grab a coat when I saw the little cherubic bundle tottering along, I went to a house where I'd seen several children before, but no adults. They were unsociable, and I'd always wondered if it was language-related or cultural, as I had seen a number of women in Middle Eastern dress.

Bouncing and jiggling the little guy to try to keep both of us warm, I rang the doorbell and waited. I rang it again and waited. Rang it yet again and, *finally*, an annoyed man answered the door, snatched the baby from my arms, and closed the door without any eye contact and without saying a word! So strange. Freezing, I hurried home and prayed for the lives of the peculiar household's children. During our life in the city, we met lots of unusual people with very different lives than we had ever witnessed.

One thing all our neighbors had in common was our disdain for the poor-quality city schools. Nobody used them. Most people sent their children to private schools.

Dave and I had put all of our kids into Christian schools years earlier, feeling our money was better spent on early Christian education foundations than being socked away for college someday in the future. We chose to trust God to supply the need for college money when the time came. The Christian school was a bit of a drive, but we had been taking the trek for quite a while, and it was immaterial that the drive was now 35 minutes from the city rather than 25 minutes from the suburb. The kids were all settled, had friends, and loved their teachers and school. By keeping them at the same school, we felt the one solid constant would be helpful in their transition to city living since not *everything* changed.

Amusing Anecdote

We drove the kids to school because we had decided to keep them in Bible-based Christian education. We felt they could be out in the world and make a difference for the Gospel later, but we wanted to shelter them from bad influences for as long as possible. Public education was increasingly antagonistic to Christian values, and Daniel had come home several times with torn clothes from playground bullies, so we felt it was best for us. Consequently, we spent a fair amount of time in the 15-passenger van, and we had quite a few comical moments!

*On one of our drives, one of the boys saw a sign on the Pizza Hut restaurant's lawn, and he said, "That's so nice they encourage their drivers to be quick when delivering pizzas. See? It says 'Now Hurry Drivers.' " The sign actually said "Now Hiring Drivers," but it was such a nice sentiment that we didn't have the heart to correct him.

*Another morning, the news was on, and I wasn't paying attention to what was said as I was attending to the road in rush hour traffic. One of the boys asked, "What does it mean when you 'grape' someone? Do they throw grapes at them? That wouldn't be very nice." Apparently, he had heard a rape reported on the radio's morning news bulletin. From that day forward, if anyone in our family encroached on your personal space, you were expected to yell "Grape!"

*Similarly, Nate saw a typical billboard campaign against drinking and driving. He became inquisitive and asked, "Are they concerned the driver will have to pee?"

*Okay, just one more van story. Two of the boys were in an argument. Daniel came forward and said his little brother was being a J-E-R-K, spelling it to avoid saying it aloud. Well, Zachariah heard him and said, "Oh yeah? Well, you're a A-F-F-O-R-D-A-B...." Puzzled at what he was spelling, I looked across the street from the traffic light where we were stopped, and I saw a sign on a mechanic's garage—Affordable

Muffler. Zachariah, seven years younger than Daniel, couldn't spell at all, but he knew how to read letters like a champ!

When Olive and Zachariah began kindergarten, they were our fourth and fifth children to attend the Christian school. Zach was good with phonics and early reading fundamentals, but Olive struggled mightily. She had difficulties with both reading and math concepts. We gave her all the support we could at home, but after her first school year, Zach went on to first grade, and Olive had to repeat kindergarten—this time with her little sister, Esther.

After that subsequent year, we agreed with the school's position that Olive was going to need the support of a public school system and the use of an IEP (Individualized Education Plan) to receive her education. It was unfortunate she wouldn't be in the same school as all her siblings, but her learning needs were beyond what any typical classroom teacher could provide with a roomful of small children to teach and no paraprofessional help.

Olive's education was definitely going to be a challenging adventure in parenting. Thankfully, God already knew this and had me exposed to the world of special education earlier in my life. Inspired by my brother's dyslexia and learning disabilities, my own mother had gotten her master's degree in special education. She worked districtwide on assessments, placing children in appropriate educational settings. She also proved to be an invaluable resource, a divine provision when I had any questions or issues.

Olive had to attend the local public school in our city district, and I became concerned it was not the best school system, not by a long shot. My mom told me I had to be diligent to ensure she got the services she needed as the "squeaky wheel gets the grease" in large public schools, and Olive was not a particularly disruptive student. At home, however, she had become quite difficult, and we were worried about Esther sharing a room with her.

Olive was very hard on her little sister as it seemed to make her feel better when she knocked Esther down a few pegs. It wasn't uncommon for me to come upstairs and find Esther sound asleep in the fetal position with her pillow and "blanky" on the carpeted floor of the hallway outside her bedroom. It broke my heart. Our oldest daughter, Sarah, ended up inviting Esther to sleep in a little bed in the corner of her room. It was so sad the two sisters closest in age, only 20 months apart, couldn't live peacefully together. We got all the emotional, psychological, and professional support we could for Olive and prayed for the best.

One day, Olive told me of a little African American girl at school who was giving her a very hard time. I inquired about it with the teacher, who was also Black. She told me one little girl really did seem to have an issue with Olive and she was keeping an eye on it but didn't know the source of the problem.

I often came into the classroom to help do various tasks for the teacher, so I kept an eye and ear open, and eventually, the truth came out. The little girl told Olive she didn't like her because her mother "was blue." Like a Smurf?! I was initially stumped but then realized this little girl had perhaps only seen White people from afar, not up close—and I have very blue eyes. That was it. Plain and simple prejudice, judging someone by their outward appearance, in a little five-year-old girl.

Prejudice and racism were pretty regular topics of conversation in our household as we had to absorb ignorant comments, looks of disapproval, and at one time, a real estate transaction even our realtor thought was being blocked by racism. It was sort of edifying for the kids to see I was being judged for my eye color, and they got to see prejudice can be a two-way street. It was so hard for them to fathom that someone didn't love their mom, who was only trying to help out in the class, let alone dislike her for her eye color.

The school did the best they could for our daughter, but in the end, we had to remove Olive from the public system because, similar to the Christian school, they were having no success in advancing her education, even with an IEP. Fortunately, I had found a special needs private school that willingly took on her challenges! I was so excited when I found a place whose mission it was to *specifically* teach children with special needs—those who often slipped through the cracks in traditional education settings. It was a Catholic school run by the Sisters of Notre Dame, and according to my dad, the Boston Irish Catholic former cop, "If those Notre Dame nuns can't get it done, no one can!"

Amusing Anecdote

Our daughter Olive had significant cognitive issues, but we always tried to keep levity in the situation when she seemed confused with her word choices. She had dyslexia and would pronounce "nail polish" as "pail nolish," and our whole family called it that!

Some of her word scrambles were cute, and others would tear your heart out; just like the time I was driving her to her school while Michelle drove all the other kids 25 miles in the other direction, and it was just me and Olive. We were talking about school, and she mentioned how often she gets "mixed fused"—the poor thing even jumbled the terms confused and mixed up! I didn't let her see the tears running down my face, and I kept my voice as even as I could, despite the choke in my throat. She was in the backseat of the car, so I kept my eyes forward on the road as my heart tore in two for her—and I prayed.

She inadvertently created some cute words that made more sense than the original words, and we called those "Olivy-isms." For instance, she referred to a skunk as a "stunk." Well—yeah! I tried to show her how it was spelled, sounding out each letter, but it was no use. To her, it was always "stunk." Period. Another cute one was that she referred to baptism as being "bath-tized"—again, it really was a more apt word!

So at this point, with Olive's new school on the other side of the county, Michelle and I started to drive two opposite directions every morning to two different schools that were 40 miles apart: one on the east side of Cleveland (15 miles) and one in a county just west of Cleveland (25 miles west of home).

It was quite stressful.

Dave joked he needed to buy me a Winnebago so I could cook dinner as I drove! But God was cooking up something else on His own, and it wasn't dinner. He gave Dave and I the sense that another child was coming—and our family's God adventure was about to grow yet again.

Amusing Anecdote

Olive was having a lesson in punctuation at school, and when they were learning about the use of the period, she said, "Oh, my mom gets a period."—out loud to the schoolteacher nun and her entire second-grade class!

The heart of man plans his way,
but the Lord establishes his steps.

(Proverbs 16:9)

6

Godly Number Seven

Again, it started with a dream. God was prepared to add to our plethora of people, and it was already a very full household! The Lord propelled us along in our adoption adventure through another revelation.

This time, my dream featured a little boy named "Tony," and in the dream, I told my friend that we were going to change his name. Tony Campbell just sounded off to me—a cultural combination that sounded wrong—like Patrick Lombardelli or Juan Goldberg. There is no accounting for the content of dreams, so please don't email me and tell me you know a nice man named Pierre Gonzales!

Dave and I decided to be proactive and updated our foster license at the time by doing some parent training hours downtown at Children's Services. We didn't want to have a lapse like we did with Esther when she had to go to a different family for foster care before we could take custody. If our foster license was up to date, we had the latitude to be able to do whatever the next child needed, whether it was foster or adoption.

Dave and I didn't want to be paid as foster parents, but if a child came into the welfare system who was probable to *become* a permanent custody case and adoptable, we were able to foster them until their legal process finished. No wait. This is the best scenario for children because each move is difficult for them—minimize moves, optimize the child's long-term adjustment, and improve their family bonding.

Life with six kids was going along pretty well for us in the city. Michelle had seamlessly joined the Campbell clan, and we also added another young couple, Malcolm and Chrissy*, to our family compound, inviting them to live in our carriage house. Designed for the original owner's chauffeur in the 1920s, we had a sweet little apartment above the three-car garage that had a kitchen, dining area, living room, bedroom, and bath. We became aware of the young, troubled marriage through a prayer request at church.

They were struggling because they were living with an intrusive relative while they couldn't afford their own place. We were more than happy to offer the apartment, and instead of rent, Mac mowed the lawn and did some other odd jobs for us. The kids loved having them around, and they seemed to enjoy life with the Campbells, where there was never a dull moment. God once again provided us with adult help for our household needs, which sometimes got out of hand due to Dave's regular business hours. Plus, my husband's heart's desire was to be an engaged dad when he did get home from work, rather than dealing with a chore list.

One morning, we got a call from children's services because an abusive foster home needed to be broken up. They had received a call due to mistreatment and neglect in the home, and they wanted us to consider parenting one or more of the four children—the two *oldest* of the four were almost three and two years old, respectively. They were

*Name has been changed for privacy.

very bonded because they had watched out for each other while the woman in charge of the home was otherwise occupied "caring" for the 10-month-old baby and a newborn. I'm sorry, but I had to put "caring" in quotation marks as ligature marks were found on the ankles and wrists of the 10-month-old, so I wouldn't call it care. Both boys had special needs, and Children's Services was going to have a staff meeting on all four children that same day. So we waited.

It amazes me how time slows down to a crawl when a promise from God is just coming into sight! Dave was at work, so a good friend, another adoptive mom, came over and waited out the day with me. We tried to take our minds off it, and we talked about anything and everything we could think of, but we caught ourselves repeatedly glancing at the wall phone, waiting for it to ring. Seven excruciatingly long hours later, we received a late-afternoon call.

The county decided to separate the two older boys as they felt the elder of the two might never adjust back to being a child if he was still concerned about the little one. Though in this case, the two boys were unrelated, this often happens with sibling groups. When a child has had to become parent-like and responsible for food and safety, they often have difficulty reverting to childhood—they can't let go of the caregiver role even after the danger has been removed.

The Department of Children's Services decided to give us the older of the two boys, and his name was Deshawn Anthony, though he was just called Sean. I turned to my friend and said, "But Dave and I plan to change the middle name," and she reminded me of the dream. She said, "Remember?! Tony?!—this little guy's middle name is Anthony!"

Oh. My. Gosh!

She was right!

In the stress of the moment, I'd forgotten!

The name similarity was truly confirmation; it all lined up with the earlier dream—this was indeed God's will.

We always gave our adoptive children names that helped knit them to the family. We decided to stick with "Sean" because it was best for his own sense of self, and he had the name for almost three years, but we later gave him my father's name, Paul, as his middle name. Although Zachariah and Olive had names preordained by God, we gave them family-based middle names; Zach had John, my grandfather's name, and Olive had Rose, which was my grandmother. Esther's middle name was the same as her birth mom and the same as her much-adored big brother, Daniel.

We brought Sean Paul home on a silent, snowy December night. The house was ablaze with the pre-Christmas season, and his new siblings were ecstatic, chomping at the bit to meet him. They were all bundled in snowsuits, playing out in the snow when I pulled into the driveway with their new little brother. They swarmed the car, taking Sean in like an amoeba—he was surrounded, drawn in, and became one with the whole. He was now a Campbell kid.

The little guy had a close-cropped Afro with a pathetic too-small knit beanie hat that had a hole, and he wore a threadbare coat with a big, chunky metal zipper, looking like it had come forward in time from the 1950s era, Beaver Cleaver style. He had little glasses that cupped his ears forward because he'd outgrown them quite a while back. I made a mental note, as those all-important glasses needed to be dealt with as soon as possible. He wore a bemused though somewhat vacant look as if he was in a dream. He was in his third home in as many years, but we would get this little one some reasons to smile as soon as we could, making it plain to him he had arrived in his forever home.

Trisha's Tangent

The night Sean first came home, a church friend was visiting the couple in the carriage house. She saw me pull into the driveway as the kids surrounded the car. She came down to the house with Mac and Chrissy to see the little guy (of this I have no recall as I was focused on Sean). She later relayed to me how she was brought to tears by the way he was enfolded into the Campbell family. She said that she expected us, as parents, to be warm and attentive, but it was the children who brought her to tears—upon arrival, they just fully loved him immediately as one of their siblings.

We had pizza upon arrival because we knew that nothing says celebration to young children like pizza for dinner! However, we quickly realized Sean was like a hungry puppy who had no idea when to stop eating. His ravenous appetite was a silent witness to the food deprivation of his former home. After he had eaten half a large pizza—half!—we called it quits for him. He couldn't stop himself. We suspected other issues would arise as we commenced life with this little guy, but he was quite conspicuously underfed. It took awhile, but the knuckle dimples I love on small children eventually showed up on Sean's hands.

My mommy radar was up and running on high sensitivity as I rated, assessed, and prioritized the needs of my new young son.

We took his garbage bag full of possessions, such as they were, and placed them neatly and carefully in his new bedroom dresser drawers. We weeded stuff out as each child adjusted and became more comfortable. We learned with our earlier children to throw nothing away until we had given a new child time to acclimate, and we understood the relative importance of their various things. That one item that might look like a rag to most people could also be the only thing left from their original birth home! You just cannot know.

One other thing we knew we had to contend with showed up out of the blue when we first signed the papers for Sean's foster placement. A bold notation stood out at the top of his file, and it had not been disclosed to us on the phone. In the upper corner, **MR** (mental retardation) was boldly ink stamped in bright red bold letters.

(The term "mental retardation" is no longer considered appropriate but was still commonly used in the 1990s. Nowadays, it's known as "cognitive disability" or "developmental delay," though I dislike the latter term because it implies some kind of impediment with a potential to catch up, which is untrue. This term caused considerable heartache for our daughter Olive, as she believed we were failing to help her "catch up.")

Caption: Family picture with 7 kids: Front row: Olive, Zachariah, Sean, Nathan, Ester. Back row: Daniel, me, Dave and Sarah.

I inquired and was told Sean's retardation was mild but would be life-long. His caseworker said he was in a special school and class for kids with mental retardation and developmental delay. (MR/DD)

As I held him throughout the requisite mountain of county paper-work, he had a plastic dolphin he put in and out of a paper envelope repeatedly. He was much too easily amused by this game and far too patient for an almost three-year-old forced to be in an office setting with paper-shuffling adults he didn't know. Dave and I prayed about it, and even though we saw something was not quite right, we trusted it was *not* MR, despite the social worker's admission. Thankfully, God gave us complete peace relative to signing papers for our new son, regardless of his issues, both disclosed by the county and those they left unmentioned.

The first week he was with us, I went down to his special needs classroom to see what I could glean from observation through a two-way mirror that was installed in the classroom wall for just such a purpose. I also read further into his early childhood record and found he was the eighth child of a crack cocaine addict. She was partying at Christmas time and caused him to be born over a month premature. She was addicted to crack and had a venereal disease, syphilis. Though he was to be full term at the end of January, he was born on Christmas Eve. The county was supposed to take immediate custody at birth, but his case somehow fell through the cracks during the holiday season—no pun intended.

A year and a half later, Sean's older siblings regularly arrived at school hungry, dirty, and underdressed for the weather. So, the county was called, and the entire household of children was taken into protective custody. There were eight kids, but the family should have had nine as a three-year-old brother had tragically been hit by a truck and killed on the heavily trafficked street by their house.

Reading this file made my blood boil. The mother may as well have been driving the truck herself as her three-year-old little boy was truly a victim of her distorted view of parental responsibility—or lack of it. Why was no adult holding a three-year-old's hand?! She was more concerned with her next drug fix than the care of her young, unsupervised, underfed, unloved children. I was really infuriated.

When the county arrived to take custody, Sean was the youngest child and found listless in a crib, barely responsive to human interaction at 18 months old. The mother's neglect was so severe, he was incapable of even sitting, never mind walking, due to his extraordinarily low muscle tone known as "hypotonic trunk." The intake workers surmised he had not been held or even out of the crib very much, which accounted for his severe motor coordination delays. Like Sean, his siblings fared poorly from neglect of the most basic human needs, but the older kids had also sustained a myriad of abuse. We thanked God our son was spared from some of the mistreatment his biological brothers and sisters had endured.

Seeking to make an immediate improvement in his life, we got our little boy new, bigger, and stronger glasses—they were very thick, quintessential coke-bottle lenses. He was designated by the eye doctor as "legally blind" because, without corrective lenses, he was unable to see an object unless it was actually touching his nose. The new glasses made a significant change, but my mommy radar insisted there was definitely something more profound educationally and with Sean's perception of the world.

When he woke up in the morning, he just stared at the ceiling and didn't move. We told him he could get up and come down for breakfast, but we regularly had to physically go get him. He just laid there and wouldn't move. He also had some odd stimuli he liked, such as crashing his tricycle on purpose or eating things no one else considered food. The first time I had him helping me make a pot of soup, I asked him to peel the foils off the bouillon cubes because the occupational therapist told me it's a good way to strengthen fine motor skills. He popped one in his mouth before I could stop him and made a yummy sound—he genuinely liked it! Yuck!

I started to read books, looking for clues about these odd behaviors when I came upon *The Out of Sync Child* by Carol Stock Kranowitz. Eureka—this was my boy! It was all about children with sensory processing disorder in which the central nervous system misinterprets messages from the five human senses.

We took him to the Cleveland Clinic Children's Hospital to be tested, and he was diagnosed with PDD-NOS, Pervasive Developmental Disorder-Not Otherwise Specified, a higher-functioning form of autism. The sensory integration dysfunction was an integral part of it, along with ADHD, coordination, and perception issues. It was as if all his senses needed extra stimulation; he needed extra-strong flavors to taste (similar to the bouillon cubes, he liked *hot sauce* and not chocolate sauce on his vanilla ice cream), and he loved deep compressions (strong hugs calmed him, and that was why he liked how it felt to crash his tricycle).

Finally, we found out what we were dealing with, in addition to his acute nearsightedness, and it was thankfully *not MR*. I was fascinated when the doctor told me, given Sean's history, that his autism may have actually *protected* him from some of the neglect damage that could have manifested with a typical (non-autistic) brain's development. She did feel proper parental input would have been helpful, especially if he'd had earlier therapeutic intervention, but he was thankfully out of those dark woods of neglect now.

God is so gracious to prepare us for what is coming, and we were not 100% up to speed on Sean's autism diagnosis, but we at least had dealt with several special needs learning issues. We added physical, occupational, speech, and sensory integration therapies to Sean's weekly regimen—to remediate some of the deficits caused by his pre-Campbell early childhood. It was a lot, but we had a wonderful tribe of therapists who worked with Zach and Olive, so they gladly rolled Sean into the Campbell clan schedule.

The county had placed him in his MR/DD class and initially would not allow us to withdraw him. But once we got the new diagnosis, they could no longer block our advocacy for a new class. He needed to see typically developing children so he could emulate their behavior rather than the atypical behaviors found in his MR classroom.

We tried to enroll him at the private special needs school where we had Olive, but they said his impulsivity score was too high on his assessment, so he needed to go to public school. Still in the city of Cleveland, we were in a district that had an overload of special education kids, and I wasn't at all hopeful after my earlier experiences with Olive in their system.

We got him into an early intervention class in the Cleveland public schools, and I have to admit, I was pleasantly surprised at the care and services he received at the preschool level. When he reached school age, I was already acquainted with the staff at the school that had failed to help Olive—and again, we had some significant issues.

Amusing Anecdote

In the basement of every house we ever owned, the boys set up their sports arena, which included hockey nets, basketball hoops, pucks, sticks, rackets, and balls of all shapes and sizes. They were always sports fanatics and competitive to a fault. Their sisters steered clear of their sports domain.

But, when their brother Sean showed up, their usual system had to change a bit. His coordination was slow and imprecise at best. When we taught him to ride a tricycle, we had to literally duct tape his feet to the pedals because he just couldn't replicate the forward motion needed for pedaling. His feet kept sliding off, left and right. Descending a set of stairs, he looked like an out-of-control marionette with overly loose joints; he bounced and jiggled his way down, while giving any unfortunate witnesses big hits of adrenaline, especially my mother-in-law!

I honestly wondered if I should put a helmet on him, just for day-to-day life, as I often witnessed his head barely avoiding collisions with kitchen counter corners when he rounded them at his uncoordinated full speed. But, somehow, he remained unhurt. Dave and I joked that he had countless warrior angels looking out for him—and they were all on combat pay!

But I digress. Back to the boys' indoor sports in our basement. Despite his lack of coordination, Sean was super enthusiastic and wanted to play with them. So, his big brothers created a new system to include regular intermissions when they played a brand-new sport called "Pooky-ball." ("Pooky" was a nickname designated for Sean by his brothers when he was a preschooler.) With Pooky-ball games, they didn't acknowledge any out-of-bounds areas. The ball careened anywhere and everywhere—it hurtled off the walls and even blasted off the ceiling! They had no rules—other than getting the ball to Sean and letting him have as much fun as possible.

This revealed a lot about the tender hearts of his kind big brothers. It also made it easier for Sean to sit and watch because he knew, at some point, any minute, they could yell, "Pooky-ball!" and he would be called in to play.

Sean's custody had yet to become permanent, and as such, we were required to take him to family visitation. I was glad he got to see his siblings, but I was *so* hesitant to expose him to the irresponsible biological partier mother. During one of our visits, we met several siblings; one teen sister was already a young mother herself with two kids by age 16. So, the single-teen-impoverished-mother cycle continued as she replicated her birth mom's life. I was horrified when she sent her little sister to a hot car for the baby's formula. She produced an old, bloated fruit punch gallon jug in which she had mixed the formula. I didn't even use tap water for baby formula and completely sterilized anything a baby used at our house! I just prayed the social worker would intervene, but she did not.

Sean had been with us for several months, and at another visit, the angry birth mother got in my face and insisted I turn my son out of my lap. I refused. I told her to pay attention to her other children and give him time. I said, "He will get down when he is comfortable." But she felt rejected and was childishly furious. She told the young, intimidated social worker she had to intervene, but I rebuffed the worker. My responsibility as a foster parent was to safeguard Sean, both physically and emotionally. It was my job. He clung closer each time the birth mom came over and raged at me, her foul smoker's breath tainted with alcohol, smelling like evil itself. I was his lifeboat, and Sean wanted to stay on board!

Eventually, I pointed out some of his sisters playing together and gently encouraged him to go see what they were up to. He was hesitant but got down since his curiosity was piqued. As he approached the sibling group, the mother swooped in and whisked him away to see his biological grandmother (only in her late 40s and already a great-grandmother!). The mother gave me a self-satisfied look of "I beat you." She displayed her selfish beliefs about life—it was all about her, which in no way resembles the character of any responsible mother I've ever met.

Fortunately, when he didn't have a mandatory visit, Sean now had stability with our family. After that particular visit, I was pretty rattled by the birth mom. But Sean and I were headed to the kids' school for game night, so we went up the highway to join the rest of the family, who were already playing at the school.

As we drove, Sean sat in his car seat swinging his legs, and he started to sing some nonsensical tune in the back of the van. This was a first! He had *never* sung before, *at all!* I faced forward and tried to attend to my driving as I silently cried like a baby, resonating with the heart of my son, who had survived another court-mandated visit, and his soul was singing! He felt protected and loved, creating a new feeling for him, which was all about joy. And a song welled up in him! I had a number of memorable salient moments as a mom, and this was definitely one of them.

During this period of time, we had our large-household life rolling along, and the kids were doing pretty well. Michelle and I had become pros at various "dinners on a bun" because we often ate on the go. Maybe Dave's silly Winnebago idea wasn't so absurd—the cook-and-drive combo! We would go to hockey practices at all hours, driving to and from their schools, 40 miles apart. We would take our kids to various therapies and church activities, and we still had commitments as foster parents as well.

Dave said he was quite comfortable at our current number of (seven) children, and he didn't want more kids after he turned 40. His greatest concern was to be the youthful dad the kids needed and not be the "gramps" father at a future high school graduation. But it's not wise to give God control of your life and then give Him parameters. Truly, once you are a child of God, you're living on an eternal line! No need to paint some perfect picture—life can and will get messy, and God is still in control of your great adventure. It'll be beautiful if you give Him latitude and just let Him work—He's a master!

So, our expansive household got another phone call from Children's Services that was downtown. Sean had turned five, and he'd just begun public school kindergarten. Unfortunately, we had given away all the "baby stuff" to a teen crisis pregnancy center: crib, stroller, car seat, changing table, swing, high chair— all of it. Dave had made his declaration about being "done," but whenever someone asked me about it, I'd say, "I *think* we are done having kids, but I'm not sure".

The phone rang on an October morning almost four years to the day after the phone rang about Olive. The social worker told me our daughter Olive had a four-day-old baby brother in the nursery at Metro, and they wanted us to parent him.

WHAT?!

My heart skipped a beat. I was crazy excited but felt somewhat broad-sided too. This day started out like any other, a bit hectic, but typical and then *boom*. God threw in a left-hand turn!

Amusing Anecdote

When the children were small, Dave and I used to take them on what we called "mystery tours." They were told to get in the van and buckle up for a trip they knew nothing about. As the trip progressed, they were to watch for signs and clues, so they could possibly guess where we were headed.

Sometimes a mystery tour was a day trip in Ohio to a state park, apple picking at an orchard, or even an Amish Country adventure. Other times, it was overnight or a weekend, like the time we all drove to Niagara Falls. They were really mystified on that one because we just kept driving and driving. Little did they know, Michelle and I had packed weekend bags for everyone, and they were hidden in the way back of the van. We were crossing the bridge into Canada when the kids who were able to read finally figured out our destination!

I think the most memorable mystery tour was in early December when we took the kids to see the city of Chicago, all dressed up for Christmas. Michelle and I had packed their bags when the kids were at school. Unfortunately, Michelle had to work that weekend and couldn't join us, so we used her as the ruse.

We said Shell was going on a trip and we all needed to go to the airport to say goodbye. No one batted an eye at our story because our oldest was still just 11 years old, and they were accustomed to being dragged on all errands since they were too young to be left alone in our big-city neighborhood.

We pulled up to the airport curb, and I jumped down from my seat to give Michelle a big hug "goodbye." Again, nothing unusual from the kids' viewpoint. Then, Dave and I yelled, "mystery tour!" and told them all to get out of the van. At first, they thought the airport itself was the destination, then Michelle and Dave began to pull bags from the back as I unbuckled Sean from his car seat. The kids were perplexed. Then we told them *they* were going on an airplane, not Michelle. Pandemonium broke out, right there at the curb—lots of cheering, hugs, and jumping up and down. Most of the kids had never flown.

Sean had recently joined the family, only a week earlier, but we didn't need another ticket because he was under three and could travel on my lap. Thank goodness because when we planned the trip, we didn't even have Sean on the family radar yet!

As a large family, we were splashed all over the plane since it was impossible to get nine tickets together. We assigned a younger child to each big kid and hoped they'd be okay for the short flight. I had little Esther next to me as she is a bit more prone to anxiety, and Seany-boy was ensconced in my lap.

At one point in the flight, we experienced some turbulence, and the plane jolted and made a sudden jarring drop. Daniel yelled from someplace in the cabin, forward and right of me, "Mom! That scared the crap out of Zachariah!" Thankfully, his declaration alleviated the anxiety for most of the other passengers as they all erupted in laughter.

We had two completely full adjoining rooms in a big, beautiful hotel, ate out all our meals, and took lots of taxicab rides. (We had to take *two* taxis everywhere we went.) It was a wonderful weekend—we saw the Christmas lights and sights in the city, visited a jolly old Santa, saw the Beluga whales at the Shedd Aquarium, and made wonderful family memories on that particular "mystery tour." But for all the boys—the plane rides were their favorite part!

Now to Him who is able to do far more abundantly
than all that we ask or think ... to Him be the glory....

(Ephesians 3:20–21)

7

Crazy Eight: Bubba

It was an out-of-the-blue autumn phone call. We had a typical, chaotic Campbell morning, which meant getting seven kids out the door by 7:45 in their school uniforms with full tummies, with their homework, knapsacks packed with lunches, all the pearly whites scrubbed, and the crew buckled into the van. Michelle pulled out of the drive with the crew, and I was left with just Sean, waiting to be picked up by his public school bus. Then the phone rang. Assuming it was a teacher trying to catch me before starting her school day, I picked up the phone, wondering which child would be the topic. It was Children's Services. A *new* child was the topic. They wanted to expand our gang to eight kids. Eight!

The social worker said Olive had a half-brother in the Metro General Hospital nursery, and they wanted us to parent him. It felt a bit like a sales pitch, but she went on to explain based on the mom's drug use history alone, the county was confident they would get permanent custody of Olive's little brother in just 90 days. No long, drawn-out foster child case with all the multiple complexities involved. Our daughter's birth mom had lost custody of each of her three children born over the eight years since Olive. But they needed us to get the baby out of the hospital *now*. The staff in the nursery was adamant, at four days of age, he had overstayed his welcome.

I called Dave; we excitedly talked and prayed, and he repented for saying he was done having kids. Obviously, God wasn't finished yet! Then I left for downtown, hurried and manic. God was on the move, and so were we. Like each Wednesday, we had our weekly Bible study meeting at our house that night. With no time to cancel, Dave stayed home from the hospital and took care of the study while I went to town to manage the custody paperwork and the baby pickup.

I arrived on the Metro Hospital nursery floor a bit flummoxed because I had to look for a social worker I had never met. I finally found her, but her behavior really raised my eyebrows. She was uncharacteristically flighty for a social worker—unsure of herself, running to and fro, uncertain about how to complete the paperwork. Instead of partaking in her anxious confusion, I found the nurse's station and told them I was the foster mom. So, they showed me the room where "Baby Boy County Custody" was located.

I didn't want to wake any of the little babies, so I tiptoed in and peered down into his little bassinet where I was met by a wide-awake pair of mother-melting big brown eyes above darling little dimpled cheeks. He appeared to be healthy, alert, and he had a good birth weight. I brought my face low so his blurry newborn eyes could see me, and he opened his gummy baby mouth in wonder at this new face entering his life. I immediately noted, as only a mother who had seen a lot of babies could do, he was tongue-tied. I inquired of the nurses, and no one else had noticed. I put on a gown and picked him up. As I nuzzled him with my cheek on his downy little head, I whispered into his ear, promising from this day forward, "*You*, little man, will be noticed and cared for with all that I am."

The social worker finally had her act together. I signed the county papers, and she took off without a backward glance. I felt like she hadn't even registered my face in her mind—just flighty. But I chalked it up to her oversized caseload and figured I'd get to know her during the baby's foster care period. I went to take the baby home, and the hospital said I couldn't leave because *their* paperwork needed to be completed by the now-absent *and* absentminded social worker!

Frustrated and so glad I'd thought to ask for her card, I pulled it out to call her back to the hospital. When she returned, she began acting kind of ticked off, but it wasn't my forgetfulness that required her return! I'm just the one who called—don't get mad at the messenger! She completed her paperwork, and I was *finally* allowed to leave the hospital with our newest son.

When I arrived home with the baby, I came into the living room and slid him onto Dave's shoulder like a hand in a perfect-sized glove. Ever the proud papa, he smiled down at his new son who snuggled into his neck, and Dave continued the study, his big hand cradling the baby's bottom. Of course, every heart melted with a newborn in the room, but my husband, a stickler for being orderly and thorough, finished the study. Then the loving reception of the newest Campbell baby boy commenced.

The Bible study spread the word throughout our church body—"There's a new baby at the Campbells!" I mentioned earlier how we had given away all our "baby stuff" to a crisis pregnancy center. Well, I believe the study group must have shared with others our state of unpreparedness because the next day, *everything* we needed walked right in our front door. I received calls from all over town with innumerable offers of furniture, strollers, high chairs, playpens, and all manner of baby necessities. The people of God stepped up and provided more than we could possibly have imagined, and we never even asked.

We decided to name the new baby Jonathan David. They were covenant friends (1 Samuel 18) in the Bible, and David is his adoptive dad's name, so the combination met our criteria for a name with family connection.

I tried nursing Jonathan due to his newborn age. I nursed him when he was hungry to get the most stimulation in order to get the lactation to flow again. Then I fed him some formula to ensure he got the nutrition he needed. Since we had no advanced notice of our son's arrival, I wasn't able to pump to stimulate the system like I had done before Esther's birth. In the long run, I needed medical intervention from our family doctor. (He gave me a medication that had the side effect of lactation—even in men!) But my milk came in—up and running *again* within the month—and this was the second time I got to nurse an adopted child—Esther was the first.

We had our first home visit from the baby's caseworker, and we seemed to hit it off just fine—right up until we didn't. At the beginning, her visit was cordial, but as time wore on, I realized she was emotionally drawing away. My lighthearted comments about the baby's development were met by disengaged stares. We honestly don't know when her attitude toward us changed, but at some point, she decided she did not want an African American child in our Caucasian-parented home—even though his half-sister was one of several sibling faces of color. The county is supposed to be a teammate to the foster family, but somehow, during our first home visit, the caseworker decided she was no longer on our side.

I really do understand the hesitancy of Black social workers; it's natural. They are worried about prejudice, hair and skincare struggles, and the general perception of society. But at this point in time, the

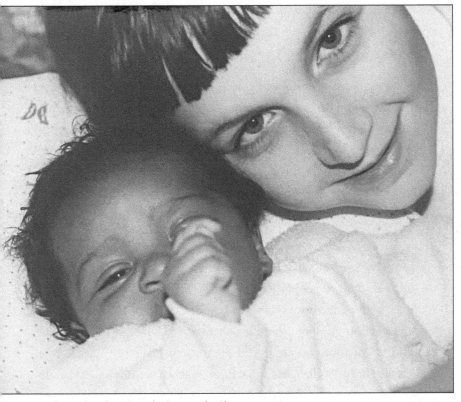

Nathan and newborn "Jonathan" soon to be Chris.

numbers support placing kids of color with White families since only 15% of adoptive families are people of color, and disproportionately, 85% of the kids in foster care are children of color. Plus, I managed to learn a great deal about our kids' skin and hair care—not intending to alleviate the social workers' concerns, but because I wanted to properly care for our children! After a bit of practice, I became quite good at haircuts and comb-outs, plus I was a speedy hair braider and beader. Ironically, I had a Black woman at church ask *me* to teach *her* how to create dreadlocks for her daughter! I did her whole head the first time, just to teach the mom, and she was able to maintain it going forward.

Despite my abilities with skin and hair care, we began to witness a downward change in our social worker's demeanor—she became genuinely adversarial.

What we didn't realize was she had prejudice against us to the degree that she would do something unprofessional. I had mentioned earlier the county would get full custody of the baby at 90 days, so we were to foster only a short time and then adopt. When we got to the assigned court date, the judge threw out the case because the social worker had filed it on day *91*—one day too late! Dave and I saw it as intentional as she could have filed on any day from the day he was born until his 90th day of age.

The social worker on Jonathan's case was a Black woman. She was under the gun to get him removed from the hospital and placed in a home because the nursery wanted him out. She did her best with the sales pitch to me about the short foster period, and she seemed quite pleased when we got him out of the nursery. But when the pressure was off, she had a change of mind or heart about our multiracial family with White parents. We were in for a whirlwind of stress for both us and our little baby.

Since the county did *not* get custody in 90 days, we now had to attend more hearings on our baby's case, and the county could choose to create a reunification plan for the birth mother. And they did—just as we feared the social worker had intended all along.

As a nursing mother, you can just imagine the stress the county's flip-flop behavior put me through. Jonathan and I had been nursing for three months, so the mother-child bond was complete; he was our son, and someone wanted to take him away. At the subsequent hearing, Dave and I sat in the back of the courtroom as we were not considered a "party" to the case, since we were "just" the foster parents.

We quietly held hands, relegated to the far corner of the courtroom like banished children in time-out. Dave's troubled eyes were glued to the front of the courtroom, his mouth compressed in concern. I looked to him for reassurance, and he occasionally turned to my pleading gaze and tried to smile. I thought I couldn't breathe, like the air had been sucked from the room, but inadvertently, I held my breath due to anxiety. The legal suspense about my baby's fate was just too much, and I didn't handle it well. Dave often squeezed my hand in an effort to comfort me.

In the end, the judge ruled the birth mother could work on her reunification plan and he was going to put a visitation schedule in place. A visitation plan! What?! No!

We were told we would reconvene in court after several months to check on her progress and the status of the case. It felt like all the blood rushed from my head, then a wave of nausea hit me. How was this happening?! But I could see the wheels turning in Dave's head, and I had faith in him and his relationship with God. If anything was within our realm of ability to influence this custody case, I was confident the Lord would show Dave what to do.

We now had to go home and do one of the hardest things we'd ever done—tell all the kids about the judge's decision and insist they now had to refer to their brother by his original birth name, "Christopher." We couldn't have him go to visits as Christopher and be Jonathan at home—it would be a formula for self-image disaster! Similarly, we couldn't expect the kids to be able to keep up some kind of ruse and not call him Jonathan whenever the social worker visited our home. We *had* to change his name, which proved to be the first of many difficult and painful changes, coming in very short order.

The kids couldn't manage the name change to Christopher, so I told them they just could *not* call him Jonathan. After awhile, they landed on the nickname "Bubba," and it stuck for many years. Bubba now had to go to visits at a county visitation center downtown that was plopped in the middle of an area known for high crime, especially drug and gun violence. We had been there countless times with Sean's family visits when he was still a foster child. We were *not* pleased to be returning.

At the onset, we were allowed to stay in the center and wait while the birth mom had her visit. She glared red-hot daggers at me and Michelle from across the open space. But we were justifiably uncomfortable allowing her out of our sight. We were well aware of her history of taking off even though she had no idea we knew a thing—the caseworker had not told her Dave and I were the adoptive parents of her daughter. For some reason, she was under the impression Olive had been housed in the Washington, D.C., area.

The birth mom's track record with the county included "flight risk." One of the reasons Christopher's half-sister Olive had such significant learning disabilities and a low IQ was because their birth mother had stolen her out of the hospital nursery. The night shift was unaware of the county's plan to take her into protective custody, and they let the birth mom take her.

The crack addiction wasn't as big a problem for Olive, but the congenital syphilis required consistent, immediate intervention with antibiotics. Since her birth mom took her from the hospital before the county, the destructive venereal disease she transferred to her went untreated, wreaking havoc on her brain. The health department finally caught up with Olive months later when her birth mom left her with someone else, but by then, the brain damage was done. Given that particular flight history, we felt justified in our concern that she might try to pull the same evasive move with our little Bubba.*

---

*Name has been changed for privacy.

After several weeks, the social workers said we had to leave and return when the visits ended because our presence was agitating the mother.

Agitating the mother?!

What about the baby crying throughout the visit?!

Didn't he have any rights?!

Part of the problem was that she held Christopher out on her lap at the end of her arm. He was used to being snuggled up close and secure near the heart. But I couldn't say anything. Plus, I was still nursing him but had not told the social worker because I knew she would have had a meltdown. My stomach twisted and turned as liquid anxiety coursed through my veins until I could return for my son. But it could still get worse—and it did.

Several months later, we returned to court for the next hearing, and the judge decided to allow the birth mom an overnight home visit. STRESS. ME. OUT. Michelle was as agitated as I was because Christopher was her baby too. She had loved and cared for all our kids, but Chris was the only one she had doted on right from birth.

An exacerbating factor for Chris was his inability to take his security blanket with him. For some kids, it's a stuffed animal; for others, a "blanky"—for Chris, it was the long hair attached to me and Michelle. If he needed comfort, he flipped, twirled, and stroked our hair, so I had no way to send *that* with him! And really—I thought about it! I toyed with the idea of cutting off some long locks and using my sewing machine to affix them to some fabric or blanket.

---

*[The ear nose and throat specialist we used for Chris said his ear issues, tongue-tie, and jaw malformation were nasopharyngeal issues from early drug use in utero. He was not drug addicted at birth, but the jaw malformation ultimately required years of orthodontia from childhood and into adulthood to fix the severe malocclusion of his jaw and a number of missing teeth.]

The social worker arrived to take him for the overnight stay, but Bubba was furious and uncooperative. Though he was walking then, he still couldn't talk but wordlessly knew what her arrival meant. He had developed a strong association—the social worker's presence meant he had to leave his mom, me. So, he fought her any way he could. First, he threw himself on the floor and refused to go with her. So, I picked him up and walked to the car with him. I handed him to her, but he would *not* allow her to put him in the car seat—he reared up and stiffened his back so it was like trying to buckle down a beam of wood.

I felt like a traitor but had to intervene to get him into the seat for the social worker. I put my cheek against his head and soothingly told him how much fun he was going to have and that he'd see us in a little while. My voice quieted him and as soon as I felt his rigid body relax, I pushed the buckle down and secured him. Immediately recognizing he was duped, he was furious again. So, I caressed his hair, kissed him, and murmured a blessing of protection over him. Then, I turned my back to avoid his pleading eyes and newly erupting heart-wrenching cries, went into the house, and collapsed in a puddle of my own tears—sobs wracked my body as I knelt on the floor.

They pulled out of the driveway.

Meanwhile, Michelle had hidden herself out on a cul-de-sac near our house and planned to *follow the social worker*! She told me she just needed to know where Bubba was taken in case something happened. It was her contention, if we at least knew where he was, we could respond more readily if and when the need arose. She followed the caseworker to a ramshackle house in an iffy part of east Cleveland. Most of that section of Cleveland is questionable for safety—boarded up former crack houses, trash-strewn sidewalks, weed-choked yards, and unemployed, aimless youths stalking the streets.

I sent a small dissertation on my son's needs, written longhand, but I was concerned she wouldn't feed him adequately due to the tongue-tie or give his medicine correctly—he was prone to ear infections. We had to stay at home, sit on our hands, and wait. Agitation and anxiety took root in my chest, and they would not depart till my child returned. The other kids were upset we "let" this happen, but we had to explain how we were not in total control of the situation—we had to entrust our baby to God's care. Prayer was the only power we had over the current legal mandates.

My concerns were later validated when the birth mom called to ask a question. In the background, I could hear Bubba screaming and the television volume turned way up, as if to drown him out. We didn't watch a lot of TV at our house, nor did we allow the television's volume to steal the peace in our home—but I couldn't make any comment. I still had no rights.

Frustrated and anxious, butterflies filled my chest and stomach—I couldn't sleep until Bubba returned home safely the next day.

After the social worker dropped him off at the house, he hugged me like he'd never let go—at first. Then he pushed back and started to hit me in frustration, as if to say "how could you?" He was just a toddler, not yet two years of age, but he had to process the complicated, commingled emotions of relief and rage. Unable to verbalize, he communicated and vented his pain, frustration, and confusion the only way he knew how.

Shortly after all this stress began with the baby, it started to manifest in some rather odd health challenges for me. One particular symptom I had was vexing—sometimes my vision "fractured." It was the one word I could think of to tell the doctors, to describe what I saw when it happened—it was as though I was seeing through a broken window or into a fractured mirror. I went through a gauntlet of testing, and they diagnosed me with exacerbating-remitting multiple sclerosis, a form of MS. We prayed and trusted God was in control, and by His stripes, I was healed (Isaiah 53:5).

A month later, they rescinded the diagnosis when a lumbar puncture test came back negative for a certain protein that should be present with MS. The doctors started to treat me for "migraine aura" because of the vision issues, though I didn't manifest the headache. I also began to have well-founded anxiety issues about the baby's case, but these too were not God's will, so we prayed and trusted Him.

Meanwhile, Dave had a revelation of how to influence Bubba's case. He had hired a lawyer to represent us, and the lawyer had made a petition to the court to give us "standing" in the case based on our being the legal parents of Olive. As Christopher's biological sister, who was bonded with him from birth, the lawyer reasoned she had rights relative to the case, and as her parents, we were guardians of those legal rights. Our lawyers brought this argument before a judge, and he decided on our behalf. We were qualified to have legal standing in the case, based solely on our status as Olive's parents. So, unfortunately, that cat was out of the bag—the birth mom now knew we had Olive.

The case was getting more and more complex, but Dave said our lawyers were hopeful about the dispute on behalf of Olive's sibling rights, and we were encouraged.

Regular life with our seven other children had to go on despite my poor health and the seemingly endless legal situation with Bubba, which droned on for years. I took Sean and some other siblings who needed therapies to a children's achievement center after school and evenings. They received speech therapy, occupational therapy, sensory integration therapy, and even physical therapy. As great a blessing as it was, at a certain point, Sean wanted to know why the other kids got to go to dance class or hockey while he always went to therapy.

He was absolutely right.

I needed the Cleveland district to step up and give him therapeutic services during the school day. And I really *tried.*

I asked nicely, at first. He got nothing. Then I vehemently demanded that the school should give him the services he needed. He was legally blind (acutely nearsighted, -18¾) and autistic for Pete's sake! My most recent observations in his classroom gleaned a different conclusion than in the past. His autism manifested in his "zoning out," which didn't require teacher intervention—they had so many other tougher, noisier, demanding behavioral issues, Sean was readily ignored. Their attention had to be focused on the loudest, most challenging child at any given moment. I pointed out the mandates on Sean's IEP (Individualized Education Plan), but they just wouldn't or couldn't meet the criteria.

So, I shifted my focus from the school and went to their bosses. With mama-bear boldness, I stormed the board of education and the Office of the Superintendent of Schools. I told them in no uncertain terms that they broke the law by failing to give my son the services laid out in his IEP, which is a legally binding *federal* document. They were apologetic but intractable and unhelpful.

Dave and I prayed about it, and regardless of our efforts, the Cleveland system would not, in fact they *could* not, give Sean the services he required to be successful socially or academically. We soon came to realize that, despite still not having closure on Bubba's custody, we had to move again.

Daniel Foreman with Chris. Buddies.

Trisha Tangent:
Difficult Conversations

We had a huge family, so it was important to create unscheduled time with each child to give them one-on-one parent time to ask us questions or just so they could feel they weren't always part of a crowd. To achieve this, Dave and I tried to include a child when we ran errands or needed to bring someone to a sports practice or lessons. It afforded us downtime we could use to train, teach, or just love them.

One such window I often used was having someone in the waiting area with me while another child was in a therapy session. As a parent, I sometimes needed to use those moments for myself, to just decompress or read, but they were also excellent times to interact one-on-one with kids too.

When a child is adopted, lots of difficult thoughts, feelings, and issues can arise throughout childhood, and they differ from biological kids. We couldn't possibly know when little life events brought up an idea, a memory, a hurt, or a slight. Being available didn't always mean we had to get into heavy-hitting discussions each and every time, but it created the avenue. It let them know that the line of communication was always open if and when they needed or wanted to talk. We opened the door; they decided when or whether to walk through it.

As adults, we shouldn't intentionally bring up difficult topics of discussion; instead, we should allow the child to do so. It's been our experience that kids will initiate a topic when they are ready to handle the subject matter. They won't ask questions when they aren't ready to hear the answer. If I barged into a subject, it may have opened a can of worms, and I would never get all those wrigglers back under the lid!

For instance, when a child was ready to ask about where a birth parent was or how they were doing, it was my responsibility to tell them what I knew. If what I knew was insufficient for them, I'd tell them I would try to find out more. We tried to never say anything bad about a birth parent. If they were in prison, I'd say so and say I was "sure they were trying their best, but they felt that they had no good choices and made a bad decision. Everybody makes bad choices sometimes, right?"—or something along those lines. We did not lie but soft-pedaled and were as gentle with difficult truths as we could be.

One time, we were at the achievement center, waiting for a therapy session to be concluded, and my extracurricular kid of the day, Zachariah, started asking a *lot* of heavy-hitting questions. He may have just arrived at a greater level of maturity, overheard a conversation that made him think, or had just been pondering. His questions delved into why his mom didn't keep him (she was just a teenager), where his dad was in all this (prison), would he be "like that" (a criminal), was there any way he could meet them, and on and on he went. It was a difficult conversation, but it went well as I stayed honest and positive all through the conversation.

Another good principle, in addition to speaking well of their birth parents, was that we always spoke of adoption itself in a positive light. We didn't say "given up for adoption" because it sounds so negative, like "I'm giving up." We used the phrase "made an adoption plan" or something that sounded like their birth parents did something responsible

Amy with Chris. I held her kids, now she holds mine.

and positive. Even if the child was taken into custody by Children's Services, we found a way to couch it to be less negative.

Another term we tried to keep positive was for our multiracial son, Zach—and we always tried to say it just that way. Some people use the term "mixed," but we thought the connotations were negative. The word "mixed" sounds like "mixed up" or "confused." The term "multi" has positive connotations because it means "many," like a multitude. We thoughtfully considered the verbiage we used and kept it positive.

Plus, I always reminded the kids that our God has different ways of getting people where they are supposed to be. I told them about when Moses got adopted and was put in position to save his entire race because of where God had placed him. I told them about Samuel's mom, Hannah, and how she made an adoption plan for her son, Samuel, and God used it mightily. I also told them about how well it worked out when Ruth lived with and cared for her mother-in-law, and they were of different races. Many stories in the Bible can help impart these complicated truths to adopted and biological kids.

Difficult conversations needed to take place. We never dodged them, but we didn't force them to happen before the child was ready to hear the answers. We stayed honest and positive and made sure they knew how much they were loved and accepted. We tried to use examples from life and the Bible, which also helped them to understand, and those conversations went just fine.

... He goes before them, and the sheep follow Him,
for they know His voice.

(John 10:4)

8

Back to the Burbs

Following God had become downright nomadic for our family. If God moved, so did we.

When we couldn't get Cleveland schools to provide autism services for Sean in our west-side neighborhood, we began to look for another house in a racially diverse school district on the other side of town, well known for its excellent special education program. Dave had gotten a new job way over on the east side of Cleveland as well! Coincidence? I don't think so! When God makes a move, He thinks of everything. But moving this huge family wasn't going to be easy. We ran into some surprising obstacles due to the racial makeup of our family.

Dave and I had found a wonderful new-construction subdivision that would meet our family's housing needs. We signed an intent-to-purchase agreement, and the buying process was going fine until we brought our eight racially diverse children to see the new place.

I was kind of sad and nostalgic about leaving the antique house near the lake—old homes have so much soul. The kids, however, were absolutely thrilled to see this beautiful, shiny new house we intended to purchase. They were running around the new house, all excited, claiming various rooms as their own. "This one's mine!" And they would shout to each other to "come see *this!*" It had a great open floor plan, a big, wide-open yard for play, and a basement we intended to finish for the kids to be able to blow off steam and be rambunctious indoors during Ohio's cold-weather months. They loved the new place, but from that day we showed them the house, we had nothing but senseless roadblocks from the developer—it took awhile to see they were just plain racist.

Items found in a typical contract for new construction, such as a warranty for a given period of time were met by a stubborn stone wall of disagreement from the developer. We engaged legal representation to try to navigate through the new construction issues, which can be a bit different than an existing home purchase. Our lawyer could *not* get the developer to agree to what was considered standard terms for new construction. Every inquiry was met with a disagreeable, blunt "no." They wouldn't even give feedback on what they wanted or how to change the verbiage of our offer. It was just "no."

At this point, we realized the timing of their contentiousness—it started right after we brought the kids to see the house. The house was built on speculation, and other houses in the neighborhood had not been "filled in"—many lots were empty, the houses yet to be built. Dave said they were likely worried our family would somehow dissuade people from buying into the neighborhood. So, they just stonewalled us—no give-and-take as in a typical contract negotiation. Our real estate agent said it was such a blatant violation of the Fair Housing Act, she offered to embroil herself in a lawsuit if we chose to pursue legal action.

Though frustrated, we decided to quietly drop the issue as we felt a lawsuit would reflect badly on the Lord. Admittedly, we were a bit surprised and disappointed in the sellers, a Jewish company. We thought they would be *more* inclined to be tolerant of diversity since the Jewish people have been the object of scorn and prejudicial treatment for centuries and still are to this day! We gracefully let the house go after we wasted several thousand dollars on legal fees. We wanted to be forgiving and Christ-like to our intractable Jewish neighbors.

We didn't tell the kids why we lost the house they loved; we merely told them it didn't work out, and then we continued the house hunt. Unfortunately, although we had chosen a county and school district with wonderful educational services for Sean, the housing stock in the area did not meet our needs at all. Most of it was 5,000 square feet of palatial living area and three bedrooms. Soaring ceilings and elegant high-end fixtures were of no use to us. We didn't need a house dressed to impress. What we needed was a functional home for a huge family with lots of bedrooms and bathrooms!

Earlier in our search, we had seen a very old (c.1835, pre-Civil War, another antique!) Greek revival farmhouse in need of a ton of restoration work. With post and beam construction, it had good bones plus lots of space—six bedrooms and four and a half bathrooms! But Dave was less than enthusiastic about taking on another home renovation project, so we continued our quest without a second look.

Then, after the new house deal fell through, I confessed to Dave I had a strong sense God wanted us to restore the old house we had seen earlier in our house hunt. Dumbfounded by my reticence, Dave asked why I hadn't spoken up sooner! But the debacle with the Jewish developer had just confirmed the sense I had about the old place and made Dave's anti-renovation qualms seem less relevant. We doubled back and bought the ancient fixer-upper. We would find the resources to make the decrepit old place into a wonderful home since God wanted us there.

Shrouded in years of tree and vine overgrowth, the driveway was littered with crumbling asphalt, mud, and kiddie pool–sized potholes.

The front walk was completely unapproachable, defunct for decades. Its frost-heaved stones looked to be certain ankle breakers, so the side door was the main entry. The house's exterior was peeling like a banana, as there seemed to be more paint off the house than on. The one garage on the property was down in a swale, without a drain, in stagnant water and rotting from the ground up. Slumped to one side and with doors hanging askew, we cautioned the kids to stay away from the ready-to-collapse, rickety old building. We had demolition plans for its very near future.

The inside of the house was not as unlivable as it appeared from the outside, just filthy and unmaintained. Dave said the previous owner's idea of home maintenance seemed to be changing light bulbs! It was evident that the house had been neglected for years; baseboard heating elements had a quarter of an inch of dust layered on top. The laundry room was in its own little dungeon; its roof leaked like a sieve, so now we understood why their washing machines were up on pedestals of concrete! The antebellum dirt-floor basement had mud puddles—*mud* puddles *in* the house! We cleaned our new place as well as we could, got the basement waterproofed, and settled in for a long seven-year renovation-restoration extravaganza.

We needed to construct an outbuilding to house a number of functions the old house couldn't provide. We really wanted to build a big barn, which would be perfectly appropriate next to an 1835 farmhouse, but our new town had an architectural review board, and it wouldn't allow us to build a barn, just a garage. So, our first huge project was a building we lovingly referred to as the "Taj Garage" (not a barn!), just a *gigantic* garage. Upon completion, the structure housed three cars, the tractor and yard equipment for our three-and-a-half acre property, Dave's workshop, and a full bathroom—upstairs was Dave's home office, a storage room, and our kids' game room.

The Taj Garage was the control center we needed to facilitate the work on the actual house. For instance, when the laundry room was literally falling down on our heads, we couldn't possibly go to a laundromat every day with our vast volume of dirty clothes, so we moved the whole kit and caboodle to the Taj while the new laundry was constructed in the house. Over the years, one project followed another until we turned the entire property into a beautiful haven.

About a decade later, after the house was a wonderful, functional blessing of a home, the girls admitted they had to resist bursting into tears when they first saw the crumbling, peeling old house. Leaving the beautiful big mansion by the lake was quite a sacrifice for all the kids, but they understood Cleveland didn't meet Sean's educational needs and their dad had a new job on Cleveland's east side as well. Life on the west side, in the Edgewater neighborhood, became a thing of the past, a lovely memory—family history.

The farmhouse was to be a quieter, simpler life, but it was without a doubt, the worst house in an affluent town—they had the highest per capita income in the entire state! The arrival of our unique household markedly changed the racial demographics as only 700 souls resided in the whole town, but we did feel warmly welcomed. Thankfully, the school district itself had excellent diversity, not just Black and White—it had a wonderful mixture of cultural ethnicities, socioeconomic levels, and religious diversity too.

The move back to the burbs was best for our family in so many ways. We didn't know we were going to need the public school system for several of our other kids, not just Sean. It was a blessing to be in an excellent school district, so when we needed to use it, we could. It gave us flexibility and peace of mind in the educational realm.

The district was also very flexible and generous with their transportation department, so we didn't have to drive kids to school anymore!

No more long van rides every morning and afternoon because the district provided transportation—our kids got picked up and dropped off at our driveway! Michelle and I were freed up to do more at the "homestead" because we no longer drove to their schools that were 40 miles apart! (This is the house where we instituted the new rule about walking to school if you missed the bus!)

Additionally, the new house was a stone's throw away from a private school with a great hockey program and stellar academics for the oldest boys. Sarah's middle school math teacher recommended an all-girls high school for her, as she was a bit self-conscious of her high IQ in front of boys. A great all-girls school was just two towns over. God had prearranged everything, even stuff we didn't know we needed!

He continued to "supply all our needs through His riches and glory in Christ Jesus" (Philippians 4:19). God gave discernment when we needed it most to fulfill His plans in our life's purpose, continuing to design and fashion the adventure to which He'd called us. And He was about to create another rather unusual feature to our journey.

Amusing Anecdote

Lying in the grass on a lazy, hot summer day, the kids and I looked up at the clouds and shouted out the shapes we saw; there's a lion, there's a teddy bear, etc. Suddenly an airplane started to jet across our viewing area, and I questioned aloud, "I wonder where they are going?" My daughter Esther sat up, looked at me like I was daft, and said, "The airport!"

We were about to get a special delivery from the airport ourselves! Shortly after moving to the east side, we were asked to add again to our dynamic family by helping with housing for the local AA Lake County Captains baseball team, a farm team for the Cleveland Indians. Our good friend from church, Jim, was the team chaplain and asked friends to house ballplayers who were coming into the States from other countries. He needed people to help them with English and acclimation to American life as many of them came from Central and South America and the Caribbean Islands. He was also required to protect them from overzealous fans who could potentially take advantage of them, if and when they succeeded in Major League Baseball. Jim called on his Christian friends to help out because he knew we would give loving care, no strings attached.

We were assigned a 19-year-old young man named Ricardo, who was from the Dominican Republic. It was quite an eye-opening experience for him but also for the Campbell kids who had lived with typical

American conveniences their whole lives. Ricardo was from a poor, underdeveloped country, and he had never seen things like a garbage disposal, dishwasher, or washing machine. We had to show him how to do many things Americans readily take for granted.

The first time I showed him how to use the clothes washer, he stood stock-still and watched it agitate the clothing. He was mesmerized. I left the laundry room but upon returning awhile later found Ricardo still there, leaning with his hands on the front two corners of the machine, the lid open, staring into the drum, watching his laundry like a TV show. How easily he was amused! I explained the machine would work without him—he *could* leave the room!

In the kitchen, when I showed him how to use the garbage disposal, he jumped back abruptly as a loud growl startled and frightened him—he laughed at himself when he saw my amused facial response to his over-reaction. And whenever Ricardo used the microwave, we had to point out to him time after time, you *cannot* leave the fork in the bowl. "No tenedores en la microwave!" we'd shout with alarm as we lunged at the appliance with lightning bolts arcing and zapping inside.

He was a very sweet, kind-hearted guy, and I loved when he called me "Ma." Motherhood can and does come in many different forms. I was mothering another young man, and he arrived through yet another avenue I could never have foreseen when my life adventure with God began!

Communication was difficult as I was working from faint memories of high school Spanish and vocabulary retained from work on the Mexican hunger project, over a decade earlier. Our son Daniel, only a year and a half younger than Ricardo, was super helpful with more complex communication as he was fairly fluent in Spanish—he read books and wrote papers in his advanced high school Spanish class.

We went to many of Ricardo's home baseball games, and the kids loved to watch and cheer for their "brother."

We were on vacation one time when we decided to surprise the whole team by showing up to one of their away games up in the great state of Maine, 750 miles from home. I leaned over the back wall of the bullpen at the Seadogs' Stadium and shouted hello to some of the pitchers we'd come to know through the host program. Their faces lit up like Christmas trees as they recognized us and waved hello to Ricardo's family! When our Dominican son came to bat, the Campbells exploded in cheers. The kids loved encouraging their big brother Ricardo.

Amusing Anecdote

We were on one of our many loooong summer drives to Maine. Maine is a beautiful part of the country, from its wave-crashing shores to its majestic mountains. We hiked the mountains and grappled along the rocky shores, then indulged ourselves to feast on clams, lobster, and ice cream by the end of the day.

My parents had retired to Maine from Massachusetts when Daniel was a baby, and it had become our pattern to go up to visit during the warmer weather months. Even in northernmost Maine, we needed to use the air conditioning during the summer, especially after doing strenuous activities like hiking or rock climbing.

Anyway, one of the kids said we needed Max to run the air conditioner. I was puzzled and asked for an explanation. They pointed at the van's air conditioner knob—according to their theory, two guys named Norm and Max ran the AC. Of the two, Max ran the air conditioning much colder than Norm. Apparently, the kids perceived Norm as a bit of a slacker, and Max was a diligent guy that got the job done! The knob had their two "names" because the van manufacturer had abbreviated "Normal" to "Norm" and "Maximum" to "Max" so the words fit on the knob easily.

Oddly enough, I don't recall which child came up with this concept, but it made me laugh, and I still think of it when I turn on the air conditioner in the car. But I just love how kids perceive the world—and I really love how Max runs the air conditioning.

Those away baseball game trips could be very trying for the players and their host families. The guys sometimes finished a game in the late evening and then collapsed in exhaustion for a long bus ride home, often several states away. They arrived at their home stadium and had to be picked up in the middle of the night. Several of the host families had banded together to help each other out, so we didn't *all* have to go to the stadium at those ungodly hours to pick up our "kids."

One night, it was my turn to go pick up the players, and Dave had to go to work in the morning. So, I dragged my heavy, still-exhausted body out of bed and headed out into the night in my van. After I picked up the guys, I was driving along at three in the morning, a warm, fresh breeze in my face keeping me alert, and I had four young Black Latino men in my van. I peered into my rearview mirror and watched them behave like little kids, laughing, chiding, and nudging each other. I smiled at God. They spoke Spanish at lightning speed, so I couldn't comprehend the conversation, but I realized, once again, God had me in an adventuresome situation I could never have dreamed possible! I didn't understand a word they said—and I absolutely loved it.

The host family program was unexpected fun for all of us, but particularly Bubba. He was attached to all the ballplayers, but he loved his big bro Ricardo and all the antics in their off-hours—they played ball, rode bikes, and learned all things American. I loved it when I looked outside and saw little Christopher shooting hockey pucks with his Dominican big brother while the other kids were at school.

Their childlikeness was so refreshing. We often let Ricardo drive our family's lawn tractor when his friends were over, and they were duly impressed. I'll never forget him riding up the driveway, chuckling and joyfully wagging his head back and forth, bouncing in the seat like a little kid! Back in the Dominican, the only thing they ever rode was a bicycle.

Each player seemed to enjoy the interaction with little Bubba too because he was a precocious athlete for his age and size; he'd been exposed to so many sports with four big brothers. They all got a kick out of playing baseball, basketball, and hockey with him. He was like the little team mascot.

Unlike his fun life at home, things had not been going quite as swimmingly in little Bubba's custody battle. The case was moving at a snail's pace, but our legal team made steady headway in building a case for the kids' rights, even as the county persisted in building a case for the mother's reunification.

I had been in contact with a child psychologist willing to testify on behalf of our children and the vital importance of their early sibling relationship. She was a doctor at the university hospital, and I met her while participating in a study of children born addicted to crack cocaine. I took part in the research program biannually with our son Sean as they studied the long-term effects of this drug's exposure in utero. The child psychologist had strong convictions about early childhood emotional bonding, and her doctoral expertise in the science of child behavior was unquestionable.

We also had a nun from Olive's school who was an art therapist with a specific focus on children; she testified to the damage that could result if Olive and Chris were forced to be separated after living together for years. Sister Kathleen was especially concerned about her student Olive, who had come to dote on her baby brother, taking particular pride in her blood relation. Slowly, but surely, the pieces fell into place on behalf of the children's rights.

When all testimonies had been taken and the judge was ready to rule, we were given a court date. Dave and I arrived at the courthouse early, ready to be called any time. We were used to courthouse delays created by emergencies that can arise in children's protective services—

the docket was often unpredictable, but today seemed even worse. We waited—and waited. Dave and I sat holding hands, trying to be patient; my legs were crossed, and my foot vented my anxiety as it bounced. The nervous energy needed to go somewhere! We saw the lawyer for the birth mom, but she was nowhere in sight. I had become used to catching her eyes, narrowed and glaring at me whenever we were in the same space.

Anticlimactically, the birth mom just didn't show up for this final court date. She had stayed sober, gone for her visits, found a stable place to live, got a job, endured regular drug testing, and burned through a multitude of public lawyers. We had run the legal gambit over the years—suffered trials and appeals, plus our case was even sent up to a higher court only to have a judge throw it back down to the lower court. Her lawyer called her home when she didn't show up by late morning and woke her at about 10:30 a.m.

Very strangely, after over three years of difficult struggle, she told her lawyer to "just give him to the Campbells."

Dave and I had become genuinely conflicted in the previous year relative to prayers about this custody situation. We felt Christopher would be better off raised with us, but we struggled with ambivalent feelings because his birth mom seemed to be trying so valiantly to get her act together. And we knew how difficult addiction recovery can be as we had several friends involved in that type of ministry. Eventually, her decision to relinquish her son released us from this conundrum. Despite her apparent disdain for me, I assume something awful must have happened, and I felt sorry for her.

We immediately went into the courtroom, and the judge granted us permanent custody after her lawyer's most recent report. And just like that, after years of hearings, visitations, and three trials, it was all over.

Our family had a huge collective sigh of relief and rejoicing in our house! Though I still had a catch in my heart for the birth mom, the relief in my soul was palpable. After years of waiting, wondering, and praying, Chris was cleared to become an official Campbell! When we got the tons of paperwork in order and were assigned a court date, we all took the train to town to legally adopt Christopher. (He loved Thomas the Tank Engine at the time, so the train itself was a treat for him.) We joyously finalized his adoption at the Cleveland courthouse.

Summer came to a close, and Ricardo returned home to the Dominican Republic for a pleasant Caribbean winter. The tension of the custody case was finally off for good, and our kids settled into their respective schools, extracurricular activities, and sports teams. But puberty was approaching for several of our kids, and a fierce hormonal storm was brewing. The tension was about to ramp up all over again; this time it wasn't outside our home's haven, but within.

Amusing Anecdote

One of our daughters had a daytime incontinence issue as a young girl. It wasn't that she couldn't hold it; rather, it seemed easier in her mind to "let a little go" in her pants, and then she wouldn't have to stop to use the bathroom.

We spent a small fortune on tests, even had her put to sleep and "scoped" by a pediatric urologist. Nothing was wrong anatomically; it was a lifestyle choice for her. So, we tried to allow the natural consequences to go to work. We hoped the odor would bring peer pressure to bear, but kids didn't seem to care that she smelled.

Then we did a logical consequence and made her clean the panties. She kept doing it. Next, we had to go with an artificial consequence, and she had to write pages of "I won't pee my pants" over and over. *Still*, she would not relent—the bad habit continued.

Finally, I decided to use a shoulder alarm that was designed for night-time bedwetters. The wires went from the shoulder, under the shirt, down the pants, and ended in snaps fastened through the underwear fabric. When the circuit was completed by moisture hitting the fabric, the alarm went off! And loudly!

Our family was on vacation in Boston, Massachusetts, and we were showing the kids the sights: Faneuil Hall, the Freedom Trail, the Common, the Public Garden—all the places of my favorite childhood memories. Our daughter wore the unobtrusive alarm on her shoulder the whole day.

While in the picturesque Public Garden with the lovely swan boats, we decided to give everyone a treat and take a ride through the lagoon. The swan boats are well known, but in case you've never seen them, they are propelled by a single pedaling operator at the back of the boat. The pedals turn the paddlewheel like a small-scale version of a riverboat on the Mississippi. With no engine, it was beautiful and tranquil as you peacefully went by the willow trees, swans, and ducks with just the gentle sound of swishing from the paddler in the back. But not on the Campbell boat!

All of a sudden, the alarm shrieked! It buzzed and buzzed—on and on—like a loud, obnoxious alarm clock. My daughter, unfazed, nonchalantly looked to her left and then looked to her right as if to say, "I wonder what that noise is?" Finally, when I realized she would do nothing about it, I reached over the seat and ripped the wires out of her shorts. Alarm off. Though we can laugh now, it is definitely one of her most embarrassing life events, and she is now completely continent!

I learned to kiss the wave that slams me into the Rock of Ages.

—*Charles Spurgeon*

9

Adventurous Chance:
Troubled Transplants

We were insulated from chaos while inside our home's haven—until now. But life was becoming increasingly difficult within our four walls, not just outside them. Several of our adopted children were entering a trying time of life, difficult for even typically developing biological kids—adolescence. Hormonal havoc ensued.

We had dealt with the childhood issues of mood disorders, ADHD, learning disabilities, and the like. But when puberty hit, it came in like a strong, destructive storm complete with powerful winds of emotion and high seas of agitation. Many of our adopted children had substance exposure in utero, and a couple had syphilis at birth, so the special needs they were likely to contend with were hidden, predisposed to manifest later in life. Adjusting to our new home and surroundings was an additional exacerbating factor.

For special needs kids, moving to a new home can be extra disruptive and challenging. They all had endured early childhood moves that were jarring to their souls, even if they didn't consciously remember the change. A newborn knows the sound of their mother's voice from utero, and if adopted as a newborn infant, they lose the comfort of the one voice they knew. So regardless of the age, future change can be traumatic for adoptees.

We had transplanted our lives to a completely new area, and everyone did their best to get used to the new things. We had to make new friends in new schools, find new doctors and dentists, meet new neighbors, and try to acclimate to our new normal.

Our son Zachariah had an extra-hard boat to row, in addition to the move, since he had the psychiatric alphabet soup of ADHD, OCD, and manic depression, known also as bipolar disorder. But like I used to say to the kids, we will always be here to help, but "everyone must row with the oars he has."

He was a very cute, curly-headed boy who grew into a handsome, charming young man. He had a sensitive, compassionate heart that pricked him often as a child. For instance, we were having breakfast in a McDonald's while traveling on vacation. A special needs adult group home had a similar morning outing at the restaurant. When our food came, I noticed Zachariah was not eating and just stared at one of the wheelchair-bound clients of the group home. The young man had a headrest, a large tray across his lap, and a man-sized plastic bib dominated his chest. I was just about to remind Zach not to stare at others when I saw a quiet tear roll down his little apple cheek.

So, I slid into the booth next to him and gently asked why he couldn't eat. "Mom, look at him," he said. "It's just so sad." I told him there were a lot of difficult things like this in the world, but all we can do is try to be helpful, accept differences, and make the most of life on their behalf. "Look at his face," I said. "He's at breakfast on a sunny Saturday morning with all his housemates, and he's happy!" My son wasn't buying it.

He was really upset because the man was drooling, and no one wiped it up. Evidently, Zach's OCD exacerbated his level of concern.

I mentioned this story because we saw the gifting in our son and intentionally tried to guide him into careers of compassion later in life. We wanted him involved with people and places that would be blessed by his heart of compassion. Regrettably, he fought us tooth and nail.

On everything.

We began to see evidence of the enemy trying to ruin his life so he wouldn't or couldn't use his God-given gift. We told him the enemy of our souls works this way and he did so in the Bible as well. He tried to destroy both Moses (Exodus 1 & 2) and Jesus (Matthew 2:16–18) when they were just babies to keep them from fulfilling God's purposes. And though we could see he had wonderful gifts and qualities that could bless the world, Zach continued his obstinacy with self-assertion and willfulness that led him down paths of self-destruction.

Unfortunately, he learned early on from well-meaning and merciful therapists, educators, and intervention specialists that he could wrap them around his finger and manipulate them to get things to go his way *because* he was handsome and charming. One time, in his middle school years, a paraprofessional trusted him and left him alone in a therapy room to "work out his anger" on a stationary bicycle. She returned to an empty room.

They searched the school and the grounds but couldn't find him anywhere. When they finally called me, they had just had the police put out an all-points bulletin (APB) on my son. He had apparently used a side door exit and ran off into the acres of woods behind the school, in winter during a snowstorm, in a T-shirt, jeans, and sneakers. Michelle left the house to drive around and try to look for him. I stayed by the phone in case he called.

We later figured out he had become manic and the therapist misinterpreted it as an anger issue. He said he just had to run because he was sure he was about to burst out of his skin! So instead, he burst out the door.

He ran through the icy woods, adrenaline coursing through his veins as if he was the prey of a hunt. He came upon a small herd of deer whereupon he took on the role of the hunter himself. He picked up a hunk of log and started to try to "bag one"—swinging and flailing the huge hunk of a tree like a cudgel, displaying the incredible strength of an individual plagued by mania. After his bludgeoning efforts failed, and all the deer had fled, he continued to run, his sneakers wet and muddy as his feet crashed through the thinly ice-glassed puddles on the forest floor.

He exited the woods and approached a road crew digging with a backhoe. He asked if he could help, and they looked at him like he was crazy and bothersome. Rejected but still manic, he ran on further. Unfortunately, his flight pattern went through backyards and woods, so the APB police patrols on the regular roads missed him.

His next stop was a house under full-remodel construction, and he again asked to help the workers. But, since shivering had started to settle in, he also admitted he hoped to get some much-needed warmth. The construction crew sent the cold, wet, underdressed adolescent next door, and the police thankfully received a call from a somewhat freaked-out homeowner. The sweet, older lady was alone and had answered the door to a young, shaking kid. She was rightfully concerned about letting him in her house. He must have been a frightful sight.

We later learned from Zach's psychiatrist that his "grandiose thinking" during this manic episode was a hallmark of bipolar depression. He believed he could kill a deer barehanded or "help" men working a backhoe when he was a cold, skinny adolescent without a coat. These were classic examples of this bipolar symptom.

Amusing Anecdote

When we finally concluded that Zachariah needed a full-fledged, medical-doctor intervention, we found a kindly older gentleman psychiatrist. On our first visit, Zach and I were in the waiting room, and the usual doctor "freebies" from various pharmaceutical companies littered the room. My son saw a little clock on the table and exclaimed, "Look, Mom! 'Pro Zac' right there on the clock—he's going to really like me!" (It was, of course, a freebie from the Prozac drug manufacturer, but Zach's enthusiasm and self-assurance made me laugh.)

We took him to many therapists and psychiatrists as we were not the type of parents to eschew the professional route. We got help wherever we could find it because things were getting pretty rough within our family! Attempts to manipulate us got my son nowhere, but it also made him very angry when it didn't work at home as it often did at school. He was bent on getting his way and was resistant and noncompliant with the efforts of both his parents and psychiatric professionals.

As Christian parents, we talked to him from the scripture as our Creator understands us intimately. He led us to a line in New Testament,

"Saul, Saul, why are you persecuting Me? It is hard for you to kick against the goads."

(Acts 26:14)

A "goad" is a pointed stick used by shepherds, in this case, the Good Shepherd. The herdsman tapped the goad along the side of the sheep or goats to make them move in the right direction. They incorporated the use of the pointed end if an animal was particularly obstinate. But can you imagine the pain if one were to turn toward the sharp point, haul off, and kick it?! Ouch! We spent so much time with Zachariah trying to show him God was lovingly guiding him and so were we! We did not want to use the pointed end of the stick, but worse yet, he was directly kicking the point (while not getting the disciplinary point we were making!). He had asked Jesus to be Lord of his life, several times, but he would not listen to us or God.

Ultimately, he landed himself in a hospital's psych unit due to another manic explosion and then a suicide attempt. Zach's manic "highs" were regularly followed by very depressive emotional "lows." I prayed the psychiatrist could find medicine to lower the manic mountain peaks and fill in the valleys of despair in my son's mental disorder. I found the perfect scripture to pray back to God:

"Every valley shall be lifted up, and every mountain and hill be made low; the uneven ground shall become level, and the rough places a plain."

(Isaiah 40:4)

Frankly, I was a bit relieved when Zach was finally taken to the hospital because I knew he couldn't hurt himself or others while under lock and key with direct, professional supervision. We continued to pray for God to handle things and trusted He would keep our son from the abyss toward which he seemed to intently march.

Even in the psych unit, he was not compliant and violently threw a chair at the window in anger saying he *demanded* to get out. I told him throwing a chair at a window is a surefire way to *stay in* and he had better listen up, settle down, and do what was asked of him. Once again, his fury intensified when he couldn't manipulate his way out, but the professionals in the psychiatric hospital could identify a manipulation a mile away. Unlike Zach's teachers and interventionists, they were far too savvy for his charm to work on them.

During this same period, we were similarly struggling with our daughter Olive, also in puberty. Being born addicted to crack and with a venereal disease resulted in learning deficits; the gap between her and her peers grew wider and wider with each passing year. Since we had a second child the exact same age, Zachariah, it was easy to see their academic disparity.

As a preschooler, she was just a bit slower than the other kids, but throughout elementary school, she lagged further and further behind. Finally, we were left with no alternative than to put her in a public school in a "cross-categorical" classroom. Various categories of disability are handled this way; students with autism, developmental disabilities, and specific learning disabilities are all educated in the same room. These classes are designed to be a haven from the typical schoolroom when a student is truly incapable of being mainstreamed due to the deficits in their IQ, attention span, impulsivity issues, and the like.

Olive's greatest efforts in life were put forth to keep up a "mask of typicalness." Because she didn't look or sound like she had deficits, she often got away with it. I frequently saw her with a group of adolescent girlfriends, chatting away, and they'd erupt in laughter. Olive's blank face, not understanding whatever the joke was, would manufacture a fake laugh just a microsecond later. The girls didn't notice, but it broke her mom's heart.

And it wasn't healthy. She lived in a la-la land relative to her cognitive disability. She said she just wanted to "be normal," and then the school placed her in a class with many children that were visibly disabled and "different." This rocked her self-perception to the core.

We had spent countless hours talking about everyone being "smart" in different ways, and "school smart" wasn't the only *kind* of smart. We did lots of fun activities at home that didn't require her to have an advanced ability to read or do math, but sometimes I wonder if we may have set her up for this disappointment. We tried to make home a haven away from all her issues, but she could never escape herself. Maybe we *should* have been completely real about her learning deficits, especially at home.

When we moved her from the private school to a public one, they placed her in the correct grade for her chronological age. She went from third grade, where she struggled with late second-grade work, to being put into fifth grade because she was 10. In her mind, she had skipped fourth grade "because she was smart" and bragged about it to anyone who would listen! I tried to explain the cross-categorical concept and what had transpired, but she wouldn't have it. In her mind, what I said just *couldn't* be right. Then she arrived at the classroom.

It rocked her self-esteem world because it was impossible to hold up her mask of typicalness in the face of what she encountered there. Olive found herself seated next to someone who had Down syndrome and did higher-level math. Then a child with autism, rocking himself in the corner, could read at a higher level than Olive. It infuriated and confused her. Thankfully, she loved her cross-categorical teacher, who was wonderful at helping her feel special and capable.

Olive's mask of typicalness was a useless tool in her school classroom of special needs kids because not one of them cared one iota about her mask. They accepted each other as they were, with no judgments, as they each had special needs their entire lives. That classroom was a haven away from those who would usually pick on them, the bullies of middle school!

But in Olive's mind, this was *all wrong.*

She shouldn't be here!

She just *couldn't* belong here!

And when things go wrong as a child, if your mom doesn't fix it, it's *her* fault. So, I was in for a whirlwind of trouble.

Our family struggled for years with a variety of attention-seeking and manipulative behaviors from Olive, especially stealing and lying. Her thievery got so bad at one point we started locking various doors and cupboards in our home. The smallest little thing anyone left out would be missing upon return, and it was frustrating for all of us. When the bigger kids were away at college, we literally locked all their personal belongings in the storage room above the Taj Garage, safely away from her. Our oldest daughter was her particular target, as I think Olive sadly thought she would feel better or somehow smarter in Sarah's clothes.

At one point, she destroyed *the door* to the extra storage room, ripped it right off the hinges, just to get inside. Olive had convinced herself we were keeping something of hers in there. But the stealing didn't stay in the confines of our home. No one was exempt when she focused on something she wanted.

One day, she came home with an expensive pair of suede and shearling boots, and she said they were given to her by a friend. Because I'd lived with her lies for years, I told her I needed a note from the girl's mom that stated she was allowed to give them away. The next day, I asked, but she had no note. The second day, no note, and I took the boots into protective custody. The third day, she came home with a story that her friend's mother "moved to Chicago," hoping I would then give the boots back to her.

Though, admittedly, I was somewhat impressed by her savvy lies, I was also genuinely frustrated. How can she think up these extravagant lies so easily but can't think through a paragraph at school to give a coherent answer to a teacher or on her homework?!

I took a shopping bag and went into her bedroom when she was away on the next school day. I collected anything I knew had not been previously purchased by us or gifted to her. I had to get a second bag and ended up with *two* teeming bags full of shoes, clothes, and cosmetics, plus the boots. I called the high school's guidance office and asked for an appointment with a counselor. I returned all the merchandise, and through discussions with guidance and her teachers, we figured out that she had used the school's lost and found as her own personal shopping mall.

Needless to say, Olive was furious but took the correction a bit more gracefully as it appeared to come from the school. I let her believe they had reached out to me to help them find these missing items. So, the "lost and found shop" was now closed, but she wasn't done yet, not by a long shot. Nor had she learned a lesson about theft despite the natural consequences.

Olive decided to take things into her own hands to obtain the most coveted of all teenage possessions, a cell phone. This was a fairly new technology, and we had told the kids they could have a mobile phone only when and if they could afford to pay for it themselves. I still didn't even have one myself! Not understanding how that technology works, she took a girl's cell phone from school and used it at night when she thought it was safe because we couldn't see her with it. She was caught by the girl's parents who used the GPS to find their daughter's stolen device. They were *livid*, and rather than allow the school to handle the matter, they filed *criminal* charges against her at the town police department. Oh, Olive. *When* will you stop?! I was so irked, but my mother's heart also broke for her. Her victim was a fellow special needs student, so she was with those same classmates all day every day. How humiliating.

Then, when she was scheduled, Dave and I went with her to court. Thankfully, the judge was wonderful.

He told her how infrequently he saw kids with supportive parents. He told her she should count her blessings because we stood by her, even when she messed up. He said he also suspected, if he came over his desk after her, he would undoubtedly have to grapple with her dad, who would protect her. She took the correction, received community service hours, but still behaved as if *she* had somehow been wronged. There was a complete disconnect in her mind about her accountability, and we were desperately trying to let the consequences land squarely on her.

Stressful, emotional, and so difficult, but the troubles of adoptees take all manner of shapes and sizes. And unfortunately, things were still just ramping up.

I didn't find out till they were all grown up, but some of my more obedient children referred to Zachariah and Olive as the "terrible twins." Rightfully so, because they all had to live with the twins' shenanigans for many years. They dealt with the fallout at school and home, while also removing themselves from comforts that should have been the right of any child. I often found Esther asleep on the hallway floor in the fetal position. She chose to lay on the drafty old floor rather than go to sleep in her own bed as her sister railed against life, bad-mouthing her, her siblings, and her parents.

We had to put Olive in therapy.

A musty old building with mismatched furniture gave me pause when we first arrived, but our case was assigned to a kind grandmotherly woman, a very good listener.

Perfect.

The therapist had asked for my participation so she could get a better handle on how my daughter's anger issues were manifesting at home.

Were there any precursors?

Typical triggers?

Did I know any family history?

I put on file all I knew from her birth history, but I also shared with the therapist that Olive usually got an intense cross look on her face when the clouds of anger were beginning to loom. Sometimes, there was an external trigger; other times it was her own brain's creative malevolent thought life.

The therapist said I could help my daughter use calming strategies when she was about to blow up. She told Olive when I gave her our signal of brushing my finger along my nose, she was to go to her room and do her breathing exercises to settle down. A safe place for her to relax and try to think more clearly was also safer for the rest of our family too.

Back home, there were incidents when she just didn't get to her decompression place in enough time, and her anger burst on me like a hurricane breaching a levy. I wouldn't let anyone else handle her because I understood her explosive volatility, and she tended to blame me for most of her issues anyway, so I was the point man.

But alone on the frontline, I was vulnerable. The first time Olive physically attacked me, I was knocked to the ground, and Michelle had to pull her off as she struggled with me. We were all horrified when she made the huge step from recalcitrance to violence.

Ironically, Olive told me to call the police because she was sure they would want to know how terribly she was treated in our household. Upon their arrival, she told the officers what had happened, and they took her away. She had willingly confessed to striking me! But in the end, they just gave her a talk and tried to scare her straight. But it didn't work for long.

The next time she attacked me caused far more damage. She has a lower center of gravity and took me down again but pushed so hard that I flew into a wall, and a doorstop cut into my upper back. Thankfully, it was my *upper* back because a few years earlier, I had undergone extensive lower back surgery, requiring fusion with rods and screws. Everyone else in our family was cautious about my back, but Olive did not think when blinded by anger.

The worst part of this whole mess was when my mother-in-law dropped by amid the police intervention, just as they photographed my back injury for their report. She was horrified as she had been raised a genteel Southern lady, and violence had never been part of her life.

We had hoped the police intervening again would send a strong message to Olive—she was completely out of control and needed to change. Yet she continued to believe Mom was the primary source of all her problems. She wanted *me* to change.

So, the third and final time she physically attacked me, Michelle and I were working on dinner in the kitchen. I looked up over the prep island, saw her glare at me, and knew she was telling herself some malicious Mom-is-the-bad-guy story. As my mind registered her narrowed eyes, it was past time to brush my finger along my nose. I told her to immediately head upstairs, do her breathing exercises, and calm down in her room. She answered with an emphatic "no" that sounded more like a growl than a child responding to her mother.

I came around the island, took her by the elbow, and led her to the stairs. As I began to walk up behind her, she rounded on me, and her fist made a solid connection with my chin. The uppercut drove my lower jaw into the top, and I heard my own teeth crunch. Pain shot through my head, and it felt like I had bit down on a mouthful of gravel. I went down hard on my back, struck my head on the hardwood floor, and was fending off blows as she descended on me. The rest of the family, except Dave, who was still at work, ran to my aid and pulled her off. One of my sons literally dragged her outside because she had gone limp, and another one called the police. Again.

I was shaken to the core. My front teeth were broken, and my head pounded, but the worst part was I vibrated with an inner tremor that would not abate. My husband arrived home, and we told him the police had taken her to the emergency room. Since he wanted my head to be checked out, we went together to the hospital. We arrived to find the police had left and our daughter was being assessed by medical staff as to whether they would retain her in their psychiatric ward.

My head had started to feel better, and they couldn't do anything for my teeth, so after a short discussion, it was decided Michelle would take me home to try to relax and rest. Dave remained with our daughter.

After the assessment was complete, the hospital staff concluded she didn't belong in their unit. Dave was furious. How could that be?! He wanted to know why he had to take home a violent 17-year-old! He even went so far as to say he needed to go home and take care of his wife and they could do what they liked with Olive that evening. He was frustrated and angry because he *knew* our daughter could control herself since she had never been violent when *he* was at home.

The police returned at the request of the hospital and threatened him with child abandonment if he left her. Against his better judgment, Dave returned home with our daughter in tow, knowing life was to change radically from that day forward.

I was completely rattled and incapable of helping to parent her through this debacle. To keep Olive away from his shaken wife, Dave decided she would live in the apartment above our detached garage when he was not home. She could come over to the house only when he was there. Though it played into her demands, we moved all her belongings, gave her a mini fridge with drinks and snacks, and she was on her own. Just like she wanted. It went against our parenting instincts to give in to bad behavior, but I was in no condition to pick and choose what should be done.

Alas, this was extremely unhealthy for Olive from a psychological standpoint. We had to find a better long-term solution. Even though she vehemently insisted she just wanted to be independent, we knew her disabilities coupled with her tendency toward depression made full independence improbable.

We called the Department of Developmental Disabilities due to Olive's low IQ, and they told us it was "not their problem until she turned 18," only a couple of months away. We called the Department of Family and Children's Services, and their response was, unbelievably, they would not help "because she is *almost* 18." We were in another crazy conundrum, and we couldn't see a way through it; no public agency would help, and I had developed classic signs of full-blown PTSD from her violence.

During that time, when she got off the bus from school and walked up the driveway, though I knew she was headed to the garage, my heart pounded like it was coming out of my chest. At dinner time when Dave was home, she came over, and I broke out in a complete head-to-toe sweat despite the cool autumn weather and my husband's presence. Randomly, at night, I abruptly woke in fear, heart racing, hearing my teeth crunch in my head over and over again. If I had to be in close quarters with her, like in a car, the internal anxiety vibrator went on and on and on until I could get away from her. This little girl I had kept from life in the long-term foster system had shaken me to my core and, though I still loved her, I could not stand being near her. We needed an extreme pivot on how we were handling things with Olive.

We began to look for group homes that could manage her disabilities and moods because we felt the long-term effects of solitude in the garage would wear on her. It would wear on anyone. It seemed to Olive like her dream came true at the time because all she ever said she wanted to was to be out on her own. But human beings are social creatures; even hardened criminals can go crazy with lengthy solitary confinement.

Dave tried to help as much as he could, but he worked full time to cover our family bills that had become bloated by orthodontia, college, and private school tuitions all on top of our regular big-family expenses. I ended up doing a lot of the driving to visit possible group homes. The anxiety motor inside me would not turn off the entire time I was on those visits. But I *had* to continue in this search to settle Olive in her next phase of life, apart from me, whom she perceived as her problem.

We came to understand the group home system and how it worked, and unfortunately, we learned her family was not permitted to pay for her to live in one of these homes. *She* had to have her own income stream, and we didn't know how to achieve this with a girl who had a low IQ, was almost 18, and was about to finish high school but without an actual degree.* We found county, state, and federal monies available,

---

*(It's called "social graduation" when a disabled person cannot possibly meet the mandatory requirements to truly graduate.)

but we had a mountain of paperwork to do; physicals, interviews, physician recommendation forms, etc. all needed to be processed.

It took us from the time of the uppercut punch in September till the middle of June the next year to get all our ducks in a row. We got her signed up for Social Security disability income assistance. She qualified for Medicaid; there were county and state subsidies that paid for some bills, and she had a job putting clothes on hangers at Goodwill Industries. She had her own income stream and happily moved into her new room in a house with three other special needs young ladies. I made her pretty curtains and bought new bedding for her room to make it as cheery and positive as possible.

During this same period, her "terrible twin," Zach, brewed his own brand of a storm. He didn't have a low IQ or learning disabilities like Olive, but his mental illness was wreaking havoc. He had become promiscuous—completely inconsistent with what we taught in our Christian home. He ran away a couple of times only to be returned by the police when he was found asleep behind Walmart or once when an unsuspecting mother found him in her daughter's closet.

The poor woman was *in her underwear*, getting ready for work, and had come into her daughter's room to wake her for school. She heard a noise in the closet, opened the door, and there was my son. I felt so sorry for her and for what my son did in the life of her family. Our family was hurt as well, but I had long ago come to the conclusion that when my kids did something wonderful, I never took the credit, and I similarly would not take the blame when they did something awful. The humiliation in this situation was all Zachariah's, and I let him own it in full.

What I did do was start to have *intense* fellowship with God.

"What were You thinking?!"

"Where can I turn now for the next assist?"

"You said You would never give me more than I can handle! Well, You seem to have *way* too much confidence in me!"

And that is where He stopped me.

God can handle your questions and your anger, but don't misuse His Word. Many people say, "God will never give you more than you can handle," and the platitude is meant to be comforting or reassuring. But the origin of the scripture is actually for when you are tempted; God will not allow more than you can bear:

"No temptation has overtaken you except such as is common to man: but God is faithful, who will not allow you to be tempted beyond what you are able, but with the temptation will also make the way of escape, that you may be able to bear it."

(1 Corinthians 10:13)

So, this was where God stopped me and gently corrected and disciplined me. He showed me that He *is* faithful and had got us through so much and would continue to do so. But I don't ever use that platitude on a struggling friend. It isn't helpful, and it really means something else entirely. I took the correction and looked to His Word for the truth. In the 13th Psalm of David, I found the lifeline I sought.

Though David had been anointed king, he was struggling and felt very down, forgotten by God:

"How long, O Lord? How long must I take counsel in my soul and have sorrow in my heart all the day?"

(Psalm 13:1–2)

King David completely understood how I felt, obedient to God yet feeling forsaken. But God is good, and He is sovereign. When we walk in what He has called us to, He will allow difficult situations that afford us the actual *privilege* of bearing testimony to His grace. Suffering has a purpose in the life of a believer.

So, we have to do what David does next: he prays,

"Consider and answer me, O Lord my God; light up my eyes lest I sleep the sleep of death, lest my enemy say, 'I have prevailed over him,' lest my foes rejoice because I am shaken."

(Psalm 13:3–4)

We take an intentional stance in the steadfastness of God's love, grace, and goodness rather than our circumstances and emotions. It's a choice. He teaches us to trust Him, in the greatest of darkness. So, by the end of the Psalm, David's circumstances haven't changed one bit, but his *perception* has changed entirely:

"But I have trusted in your steadfast love; my heart shall rejoice in your salvation. I will sing to the Lord, because He has dealt bountifully with me."

(Psalm 13:5–6)

In the eighth chapter of the Gospel of Matthew, a big storm had stirred up, and the disciples were terrified. Jesus spoke to the storm, and it calmed down. The disciples were amazed that even the wind and the waves obeyed Him. In times like this, Jesus can calm the storm itself or calm the storm *inside* you despite the one that may continue to rage in your outer life. He did this for us throughout this difficult parenting season. I now firmly believe God will never give me more than *He* can handle.

I lifted my head, straightened my shoulders, and continued on. Our son Zachariah went on to genuinely graduate from high school, though Dave and I have our doubts about the legitimacy of his degree. The one class that he needed to pass to graduate was economics, and he was failing miserably. He had so many intervention specialists helping him it was ridiculous, but as I said, he is handsome and charming. They shoved and pulled and pushed, forcing him across the high school finish line.

On his final senior project, he had people make photocopies, get pictures developed, and buy craft supplies, doing anything he needed. Dave and I were the type of parents who gave you anything you needed, but *you* were to lead the charge:

You get the pictures to the store, and I will be glad to pay for them when they come in.

You write and type your paper, and I will be glad to proofread it.

You figure out what your presentation requires, and I will be glad to take you to the store for your supplies.

By the end of high school, any young person *should* handle themselves with a modicum of maturity and responsibility, determining whether they sink or swim. But not our son—he had teachers and paraprofessionals feverishly working to help him.

Zach finally graduated with a 59.7 grade point average in economics. 59.7?! Talk about sliding under the wire! Dave was convinced the school staff just didn't want him back for another year and gifted it to him, but we cheered like crazy people the day he got his diploma. We were the only ones in attendance from our family because, till the last minute, it was not evident whether he would graduate at all, so no extended family made travel plans to come for the event. Besides, it was too difficult for anyone else to celebrate a kid that had given his parents untold amounts of grief. But the grief had only taken a pause.

In athletics, when a goalie stops an attempt to score, it's called a "save"—our son Zachariah got spiritually saved more times than a hockey puck throughout his childhood. He liked the little Bibles and the attention he received from believers, but he adamantly remained unconverted and genuinely hostile to God.

"... Do you not know that friendship with the world is enmity with God? Therefore whoever wishes to be a friend of the world makes himself an enemy of God."

(James 4:4)

Zachariah continued his downward spiral into hell-bound living and so did his "terrible twin," Olive.

Amusing Anecdote

One of my sons misheard someone at a service counter asking for "their usual" and thought they said "Judy." So, when we went to Dairy Queen, he said he'd have his Judy, and we were all baffled. He said, "You know, vanilla with peanuts." Now, this guy *always* ordered unusual things; his favorite sub sandwich was disgusting in my gastronomic opinion: chicken teriyaki with pickles and olives. From that day forward, our whole family used the term "Judy" if we wanted a menu item we typically ordered—"Thanks, I'll have my Judy."

Thus you will recognize them by their fruits.

(Matthew 7:20)

10

Your Destiny is Your Choice

Despite several bitter heartaches, our adoption adventure bore sweet fruit. Apart from Zach and Olive, the rest of the Campbell kids led lives consistent with their appropriate choices and flourished. Not always easily, not always comfortably (and not always biblically!), but they found their way in the world and did so with integrity. Dave and I were *very* proud of each of them because they lived out the results of their own relatively good choices.

Daniel had a successful hockey experience in high school, though chose to do only as much as expected academically. He had always been the guy who loved a daily adrenaline fix, and he ended up at a college where he could achieve that end. The Ohio State University was great academically but also had sports galore, and he could play or cheer to his heart's content. He sometimes struggled with finances but did learn fiscal responsibility the hard way.

After a particularly naive use of his money in the autumn of his sophomore year, he had to sit out a college hockey season. He needed to earn money to rectify the financial problem and did so by emptying packages from FedEx trucks in the middle of the night. It was exhausting,

Everyone on the rocky shore of Maine on one of many trips to visit Nana and Grampa Keating. Esther must have been taking the picture.

backbreaking work, but he learned fiscal responsibility via the natural and logical consequences that had fallen to him. Money doesn't grow on trees! I mention this to point out our consistent parenting style with all our children, from the youngest to the oldest, biological or adopted, boys or girls. Daniel ultimately graduated with a degree in sports management. He then chose to go to work in sales for which he had a natural bent as he decided to end his penniless student lifestyle, which had grown old. Fiscal responsibility was learned, albeit the hard way, and he went on to have a very successful career in the world of sales.

Our daughter Sarah went to college at the tender age of 17, and it was ever so hard on her mama! I kept antacids in the car for the ride home as my distraught stomach needed them every time I dropped her off! From her high school sophomore year, she had her heart set on the Cornell School of Hotel Administration. Diligent and focused, she worked and achieved her goal. Cornell was extremely rigorous academically, and she was challenged like never before while surrounded by brilliant people for whom everything seemed to come easily, but Sarah remained on task and worked hard.

She was noticed by a computer professor who admired her persistence and work ethic in her studies, and he made her his teacher's assistant during her sophomore year. It was valuable for him to have an assistant who understood students' academic difficulties and learned to work through them. The position itself was an education and also generated some much-needed income. Additionally, she worked at the on-campus hotel, The Statler, to help further defray expenses. She had become a super multitasker with all her academics, extracurriculars, and on-campus employment, then graduated with >3.5 GPA, wonderful friends, and choices of direction she could take in the hospitality industry.

Nathan flourished with his athletics as a young man. He had always been quite coordinated with every ball, puck, or stick! When he was young, we had to keep his birth certificate handy because he was such a big kid and so athletically capable, his age was often called into question when playing in out-of-town tournaments.

In high school, he put his heart and soul into his passion for baseball and came close to the state finals at one point. His senior year, during the Ohio all-state all-stars game in the state capital, Columbus, he hit a powerful homerun. Dave and I were sadly stuck in traffic at the time and missed it. Later, his coach jokingly said if we went out to the field, we might still catch a glimpse of it because the hit was such a bomb, the ball was probably still in flight! Nate went on to have a successful baseball and academic career, graduating from Miami University of Ohio.

Our little Esther Danielle was "tearing it up" on the stage in her high school years. Earlier in childhood, she always joked that no matter how well she auditioned, she was cast as a "walking mushroom," her euphemism for getting bit parts. But once our girl reached junior high, her theatrical ability began to get noticed. In eighth grade, she was originally cast as a witch in Shakespeare's *Macbeth* but was subsequently asked to replace Lady Macbeth because Esther knew all her lines; in fact, she knew *everybody's* lines, and the female lead still hadn't fully memorized her part. So, with only one week till the performance, Esther was recast as the lead and went from being a witch to a queen. She was really concerned the original Lady Macbeth, a "popular girl," would be upset with her, but the former queen was so relieved she wouldn't make a fool of herself, so she was quite thankful.

Esther was cast again for a lead role when she was a junior in high school, Dorothy in *The Wizard of Oz*. Not *The Wiz*! The original version! The casting director made the right choice; our daughter was wonderful, but it was pioneering to have a Black Dorothy, and we *did* have to wrestle her dreadlocks into pigtails! One other cast member in Oz was Esther's best friend, Anna. When their junior year of high school was ending, Anna's father had a job transfer, and Esther asked if her "bestie" could come live with us for their last year of school. We love Anna and were glad to have her come join the Campbell clan for their senior year. Just throw another cup of water in the soup pot! We always made room for any child in need, regardless of how it came about. Anna went on to college and has a career as an administrator in a law office down in Texas. To this day, a full decade later, she still calls me "Mama C."

Esther went on to do a gap year after high school because she just wouldn't apply herself in the area of academics. She did what she needed to do to get by in her classes, but we told her we could not spend the money to send her to college when she wouldn't even do her homework while living with us under the same roof! She needed to find a growth-year alternative and found the perfect choice in the performance group Up with People (UWP). It cost us far more than a year of private college but was so well worth the investment. She ended up with a lead singer role, traveled the world, performed for huge audiences (over 10,000 in Hong Kong!), and grew in maturity by leaps and bounds.

Bursting with pride as we got on the airplane, Dave and I traveled to see Esther perform when the show was in Belgium. We also got permission from the UWP touring company to take her on a long weekend to Paris, France. It was a whirlwind, heart's desire tour of culture and cuisine for Esther, then back on the road with UWP. We had a ball!

Dear, sweet Sean finally did so well academically once we moved out of the Cleveland school district, we had him removed from the waitlist for the Cleveland Clinic's autism school. Sean had elementary school teachers request him for their class because they felt somehow "called" to help him. His first-grade teacher said she saw him regularly plunked in the hallway time-out chair by the kindergarten room, benignly staring into oblivion like Forrest Gump. She made note of our little guy in her heart to get him for her class the next year, and she was definitely one of Sean's greatest academic angels.

We thank God for giving him favor with several teachers along his educational path. Sean was also the only one of our kids to remain loyal in learning a musical instrument, the clarinet. Playing in his high school band, he marched in football game halftime shows, plus he got to perform at internationally acclaimed Severance Hall in Cleveland and was honored to march down Main Street, USA at Disney World during his spring break one year!

It never ceased to bring tears to my eyes when I saw him do wonderful things previously unfathomable when we first got him home with the bright red *MR stamp* looming at the top of his chart. Though he still needed intervention and struggled mightily with schoolwork, he was able to be a manager for the boys' basketball team, and his senior year, they honored him by dressing him for warm-ups at one game. Always a diligent worker, he had several jobs in high school and landed an excellent one with Costco when he graduated.

Chris was well known at every local athletic venue, and all the high school kids called him "Bubba." He was a notorious "rink rat" where his brothers played hockey, oftentimes scooping up the boys' thrown-away athletic tape to fashion into a ball and stick-handle it through the lobby with his little hockey stick. He went on to become an excellent athlete in his own right after watching hundreds of games in his childhood.

Once, when he was only eight years old, he made a double play that could have been a single-handed *triple* play. He was at shortstop, leaped into the air to snag a high line drive that looked like it was headed deep into the outfield; out number one. As he came down, he swung to his left and soundly tagged the kid who had already left second base; out number two. When he landed, he wound up to fire the ball back to first base since the runner was already halfway to second and had a shocked "Oh no!" look on his face as he turned to go back. It would have been out number three, but unfortunately, Chris' first baseman didn't even look—as typical eight-year-olds do, he was daydreaming. So, Chris unwound the throw and retained the ball so he wouldn't hit his inattentive teammate in the head.

His coach was completely astonished Chris, just a third grader, knew each successive move needed to accomplish the triple play. I was thrilled but not the least bit surprised. It was as though he didn't have to think, he just knew what happened next. But, of course, his coach had no idea how many games this little guy had watched throughout his childhood with four big brothers! *Five* if you included his Dominican brother, baseball pro Ricardo!

Chris struggled academically, like many of our kids. He had dyslexia and learning disabilities due to drug exposure in utero but persevered and was able to graduate high school. He is now looking at his options for life moving forward in the work world.

Amusing Anecdote

When I first left college, though I'd yet to meet God, He led me into the field of education. I taught social studies in junior high and high school plus I coached field hockey, basketball, and track. In hindsight, I see these assignments as God preparing me to be a mom of many, my true calling.

One year, when we only had six kids, the Christian school they attended lost their girls' varsity basketball coach, and I was asked to step up just as the season was about to start. Their coach had to move because her husband was transferred, and since it was late October, there wasn't time to search for a new coach. I'm not even sure how they knew about my coaching background, but after consultation with my family and explanation of the various sacrifices they would have to make, they all encouraged me to take the position.

Shortly thereafter, to add to the degree of difficulty, we got the call about fostering Sean, who would be child number seven. But God was gracious and faithful, and the season was pretty successful. I do, however, recall seeing Michelle chase Sean in the viewing stands a few times amid a game. The "amusing anecdote" from this period is actually more of a testimony to God's faithfulness and protection.

My 15-passenger family van had developed a brake issue, and they gave me a loaner van on a game day. The dealership's loaner van was primarily full of my own children plus a couple of my players, while a separate school van took the rest of the team. En route, I was on an interchange between two highways and started to feel some horizontal movement in the rear of the van, as if I was fishtailing in the snow, but the pavement was dry. I checked my rearview mirror and noted it was not my oft-wrestling boys!

I completed the big highway curve and started to work my way over to the roadside. I had a flat tire. Bummer. I was pretty far from the next exit and knew it would be extremely unsafe to try to walk the kids, but it was also too dangerous to get them out on the roadside due to the bitter cold winter temperature. So, I just called out to my heavenly Father because it was pre–cell phone days, and He was the only one who knew of my predicament.

Immediately, the scripture from Psalms came into my mind:

"I lift up my eyes to the hills. From where does my help come? My help comes from the Lord, who made heaven and earth."

(Psalm 121:1–2)

I looked to a distant hill on the road where a second highway merged down to the one I was on, and I saw this big, beautiful tow truck coming. It was a sight to behold with its pronounced, aggressive front grill and brilliant, shiny chrome trim. I stood at the rear of the broken-down van in my bright-red coat (you couldn't miss me!) and lifted my hand in a friendly wave, and he didn't slow down one iota; he just passed me up without so much as a sideways glance in my direction! Puzzled, I looked to the sky and said, "Really God?!"—because I was getting nervous. It was winter in northern Ohio, and with every passing minute the van got significantly colder, and the motley crew inside were getting restless. Again, the scripture popped into my head to "look to the hills from whence cometh my help"—funny how I remember some scriptures in the King James translation.

I returned to my spot in the rear corner of the van, looked up the highway, saw a small dot coming closer, and knew it was from God. I just knew. As the dot got bigger, I saw it was a truck, and it began to move across the highway lanes toward me. As it pulled over, I saw it looked like the beat-up old pickup truck from the *Sanford and Son* TV show—complete with the noisy engine, daylight peeking through holes in its rusted body, and a big, beautiful rusty tow truck crane on the back! The young man asked if he could help, and I told him my dilemma, complete with the part about the van full of children, now visibly rocking side to side as we spoke. He said he could, in fact, change the tire with them inside, that he'd just pick up the whole vehicle, kids and all!

This was such a God thing, where He uses "the foolish things to confound the wise" (1 Corinthians 1:27). He showed me it didn't matter what the outside of the truck looked like; what mattered was the heart of the person inside the truck!

"For the Lord sees not as man sees: man looks on the outward appearance, but the Lord looks on the heart."

(1 Samuel 16:7b)

The young mechanic finished the job quickly as he had originally been on his way to help another stranded driver. He asked nothing for his services. Thankfully, I had gone to the ATM that afternoon and had the $60 in my wallet. He said it wasn't necessary, and I assured him I was so grateful I only wished I had more! He thanked me and said he would take his girlfriend out for a nice dinner. I told him he had been such a blessing to all of us, and I asked God to bless him as well.

Then I hopped in the van, set off for the game, and shortly thereafter, the long-lost vanload of kids finally arrived at the high school where we were to play. Immediately, I traversed the court, all the while noticing my girls conducted the warm-ups we had practiced the day before. Excellent. I reached the bench, picked up my clipboard, and the clock ran down on the pregame. The buzzer sounded. I brought the girls into a huddle, gave them a quick explanation of why we were late because the curiosity was such a distraction, gave my game plan, and off they went. We had been there all of three minutes when the opening buzzer sounded, but we hadn't even missed a second of the game because God is so faithful and cares so much for His kids.

Your choices determine your destiny, and everyone needs to come to grips with this reality at some point in their life. Some sooner, others later, but our "terrible twin" boy, Zach, was bound and determined to try to make life work his own stubborn way. Throughout high school, he wanted accolades and results without actual work. We taught our children that "you work for what you get, and you get what you work for." Sadly, this appeared to be the opposite of our son's personal life credo, which seemed to be more along the lines of "I want what I want when I want it, and stay out of my way."

Zachariah had an opportunity to take vocational classes in horticulture, and he said he wanted to take advantage of the opportunity. We encouraged him as Zach had learned a lot by helping in our yard for years since our old farmhouse was on a large three-and-a-half-acre property that required a lot of maintenance. He was good with the weed whacker and blower, plus he drove the tractor well, easily using the hydraulic bucket lift on the front. And his OCD was actually beneficial in this type of work, making him precise and orderly. But he naively thought landscaping classes would just be an easy way to get out of actual schoolwork for a few hours every day. As it turned out, the program required real physical work *combined* with academics. He just managed to scrape by doing the absolute minimum.

But, since he did have the horticulture coursework on his resume, he got a great summer job at a country club golf course. As his parents, we tried to help him be punctual and keep him motivated to keep the job, but it wasn't easy. He seemed to sabotage himself at every turn, forgetting things, being late, and having "accidents."

One time, his boss sent him back to the golf course's maintenance garage for fuel as the crew's weed whackers were nearly empty. On his way back, our impetuous driver son crossed a green and made a sharp turn to avoid a hole. Zach rarely thought things through in advance, and he had the top-heavy gas can on the seat, instead of the floor where it should have been. When he cut the wheel hard, the can went flying and spilled gasoline all over an expensive putting green. The badly damaged turf was a costly mistake and had to be totally recreated after its untimely chemical death at Zach's hand. Unfortunately, this wasn't his first accident, and the maintenance boss was less than enthusiastic about his employment future at the golf course.

Zachariah had just graduated high school, so as his parents, we looked forward to his subsequent work prospects. College was not an option as we witnessed the number of intervention specialists required to push and pull him just to get through high school. He was not inclined toward any higher education. I discovered a special Social Security program that allowed any disabled person (Zach had a mental illness disability) to earn money *and* receive Social Security while saving toward the creation of his own business.

Dave and I thought this would be optimal for Zach. He could save up for equipment and a truck to take care of people's yards in the spring, summer, and fall and snowplow in the winter. Independent work, without a boss, would allow him to schedule things to suit his needs, being flexible for his disability. Sometimes his OCD could be a blessing to a customer, though his pickiness could drive coworkers crazy. Sadly, but consistently, Zach saw our plan as an effort to control him, and he rapidly sabotaged our efforts. It made me think of God and how we can do the same to Him when He tries to orchestrate events for our success.

"For I know the plans I have for you, declares the Lord, plans for welfare and not for evil, to give you a future and a hope."

(Jeremiah 29:11)

But Zach's greatest hope at the time was to spend free time outside God's plan with his most recent girlfriend. Her mother called us to complain about his bad influence on her daughter. She didn't want to have to raise a baby should an unplanned pregnancy occur, and she felt we needed to intervene with Zachariah to stop the teenage-pregnancy freight train from coming down the line! Dave had another long talk with him about promiscuity, which did not coincide with our Christian worldview.

He gave him a crystal-clear ultimatum: if he didn't stop thumbing his nose at our rules, he would have to find another place to live. This was a promise, not a threat. We would not stand for him breaking the rules and setting a terrible example for his two younger brothers. I hoped our promise would sound like a distant thunderhead whose storm Zach would want to avoid. I prayed the ominous threat would be enough to necessitate change, but it wasn't.

The very next week, Dave went to wake Zachariah for his early morning job at the golf course where they worked hard at sunrise. They needed to get off the course before the players arrived. Dave opened Zach's bedroom door, and the hallway light poured in. To not wake the whole house, he whispered to our son to wake up. He got no response, so he entered the dark room to give Zach's shoulder a wake-up shake. He bent down, and as his eyes acclimated to the dim light, he saw our son, sound asleep, entangled with his girlfriend.

Dave was furious.

He calmly raised his voice to wake them and said to *get up* and *get dressed.* He told them he would take her home, but he sent Zach to get on his bike for an early morning ride to work in the cold predawn darkness. The discussion would have to wait till he got home later.

Dave came into our room, turned on the light and dejectedly plopped down on the edge of my bedside. I woke up as he said, "You aren't going to believe what is going on in our house; you just aren't going to believe it." He shared with me what he'd walked in on down the hall, and I was jaw-droppingly astonished. How could Zach be so bold and so brash as to flaunt his disobedience, right inside our home?! I was quite struck by Dave's incredibly calm demeanor through this whole thing. Despite his profound disappointment, he was primarily saddened by it.

"The deep and due consideration of the infinite patience of God towards us will greatly promote the patience of our spirits and transform us into the same image."

—*John Trapp (1601-1669), English Bible Commentator*

We knew our son was about to reap the whirlwind as storm clouds of real life arrived in all their fury. When Zach returned from work, we calmly told him he was moving out on Saturday, two days from now. It was not our problem as to where or how this was to occur. He had been told what the consequences of his disobedient choices were, and we would not back down. As parents, he knew we didn't make empty threats; we never had and never will. He had been warned, and now he was about to see the severe results of his own decision to ignore our pleas.

Zach's cavalier attitude about the whole situation made me suspect he had been *trying* to get this particular response from us, but he was very naive about the quality of life he was entering. He truly *wanted* to be out of the house but also wanted to hold onto the victim card—"Look what they did to me … my parents are the bad guys." He was forever accusing others for his problems: parents, teachers, pastors, coaches, siblings, friends—no one was left out of his blame game. But his light treatment of this whole circumstance showed he had *no* idea what he was in for as he went out into the real world.

Saturday arrived, and he moved in with a janitor he had befriended during high school, but it lasted just a few short weeks. As charming as our son was, living with him was hard because he seemed to believe rules and boundaries applied to others, not him. The janitor had a well-intentioned heart. Since Zach had never been diligent enough to get a driver's license in high school, the guy planned to teach him to drive. He really went out of his way and bought a car for Zach, intending to have him pay it off over time. But Zach began to quickly undermine his friend's resolve to help him, and those plans completely unraveled.

He started making what he believed to be helpful commentary about the guy's parenting and his marriage. Like he was some expert! The janitor later told us our son had the audacity to climb *up on his roof*, where he was repairing a leak, and started to try to "straighten him out." He said Zach was just lucky he didn't throw him *off* the roof!

Another time, after our son had ultimately been fired from his golf course job and was just lazing around the man's house, the poor, tired guy came home from work and put on a TV show he wanted to watch. Zach childishly reacted with indignation, saying, "I was here first!" That was the last straw, and the guy told him to get his stuff and *get out!*

Our son was now homeless.

At this point, he did a bit of "couch surfing" on high school classmates' sofas, but he didn't have many friends, so in a short time, he was in a crowded, derelict men's shelter in downtown Cleveland. Zach made no effort to make things right with us to try to come home. He wanted to do *what* he wanted, *when* he wanted, and *how* he wanted. Stubborn, prideful, and ignorant, he moved headlong into the shady underworld of homelessness.

Back at the Campbell homestead, we prayed for him regularly and tried to leave him in the hands of God. Much easier said than done. With each foolish decision that included no effort to reconcile, the hopeless and helpless feelings bore deeper as if they were to settle into my very bones. The pit of my stomach seemed to churn with concern, but I had to continue to run our household, be a wife and mother, and just live my life.

It was a challenge.

Dave believed our prodigal son would turn, but he didn't pretend to know the timeline and left him in God's capable hands.

Typical of Zach, he met a girl at this period, and they decided they should "make a baby," reasoning it would help them both grow up a bit. This kind of cockamamie logic could only arise from an addled, immature teenage mind. As healthy teens are quite capable, they got pregnant in a short time and presented it as wonderful news! To be supportive, because what's done is done, I bought the girl a Christmas gift that holiday season. I tried to plaster a face of acceptance on my countenance, which tends to work on its own, falling with my heart or scowling with my impatience. Our son came home for Christmas, but without her. He took the gift, but he didn't dare to tell me they were quickly done with each other after only a few short weeks.

So, things were bad with Zach, and I thought they couldn't possibly get worse, but they could, and they did.

He returned to his street life and told us he was participating in some charity work. He said he "helped" with a ministry to prostitutes, run by a judge in Cleveland. Unfortunately, we found out he in fact was *partaking* in the ministry after being arrested for prostitution *himself*.

His behavior horrified me at this point, but I tried not to let it show. I never felt humiliated, as I let the kids take the blame and the credit for their actions in equal measure. But I'd be lying if I said I wasn't surprised at how low he could stoop and how crushed my heart was as I watched him do it. Each rebellious behavior seemed to join, tighten, and twist my tender mother's heart as he continued to make self-destructive choices. Grief would sneak up on me and take my breath away, and unwelcome, unbidden tears just flowed. It made me so sad to see how he readily trashed his own life and, worse yet, what he did to the lives of other people, young and old alike.

I recorded in my prayer journal for Zach during this period:

"I pray, God, for my son to have a desire for a right relationship with You and others. I pray he will flee temptations to stray from what is good and right in Your eyes. Give him a desire to be responsible and active in setting his future in motion. Help him see the error of his wrong ways and his evil habits ... they will not, they *cannot* coexist with You."

—My prayer journal, January 2011

He eked out a small income under the table at a few places in "the hood," but understandably couldn't get any traction in life as he kept trying to do everything the wrong way. He had still not reached the bottom of his self-destructive spiral, and he never considered repenting from his rebellion to come home as the prodigal son eventually did in the Bible (Luke 15).

He found yet another new girlfriend online (he really was a charmer!) and spoke to her on his cell phone (how could he afford a cell phone but not food?!) about his physical hunger, coldness, and desperation. Never one to carry much weight, he got pretty skinny. He apparently managed to sweet-talk her into his Cleveland exit strategy.

I was so frustrated! The pressure of difficulties needed to stay *on* if the natural consequences of his bad choices were going to do their work! But he received a bus ticket from the young lady down in Texas, and off he went. Out from under the pressure of his self-created homelessness.

Nineteen years old, without two nickels to rub together, he headed south to a new life below the Mason-Dixon line. But there is nothing new under the sun for the foolish man who wants to keep doing the same senseless things over and over, expecting a different result. As you can imagine, the young lady in Texas was also pregnant in a short time, and now Zachariah was a penniless, unemployed 19-year-old with *two* children on the way, one in the North and one in the South.

When the baby was born back home in Ohio, Zachariah was ecstatic! Proud and happy, he called from Texas to blow his self-esteem horn over the baby "he'd made!" He literally said that! A short time later, just a month after her birth, he arrived at the irrational decision he was *not* the father. It may well have had something to do with the child support request that showed up at their apartment down in Texas from Family Services in the Ohio county of the baby's birth!

It was absurd to deny his parentage since he had actually tried and succeeded to create the pregnancy. But the most ridiculous part was the baby looked like a sweet little female Zachariah with pigtails! Our son has an unusual racial composition of about 80% Caucasian, 18% Black and 2% Native American. No one ever guessed his true race and, if they tried, they guessed Latino, Greek, or something Mediterranean when it was summertime and he was tan. Regardless, he now identifies as Black though he appears to be Caucasian, especially in the winter months without any suntan. His baby daughter in Ohio has his exact same coloring with very light skin and hair, despite her Black mother's complexion.

The notion of rejecting his intentionally begotten daughter is ridiculous, but the county had to order and pay for a paternity test to confirm he was the father. As his parent, watching him try to weasel his way out of responsibility was both disappointing and frustrating. And he wasn't done making the whole situation still worse!

Once they had "found" him, the Ohio county services lost track of him again because he left the legitimate work world to go under the table once more to willfully evade financial responsibility for his daughter. He didn't want his wages garnished, but he wouldn't voluntarily pay the child support he owed. This was antithetical to how he had been raised, and our parental hearts sank to see the lives he harmed with each irrational, ungodly decision. Ironically, he created the same scenario for his own child that had haunted him most of his life. But this time, he wasn't the seemingly discarded kid; *he* was the birth parent who rejected his child.

Meanwhile, baby mama number two's pregnancy grew day by day down in Texas. Zach's next child arrived nine months after the first, and this time it was a little boy. They struggled big-time with so many mouths to feed (she already had a young daughter too) and very little income. We told them we wouldn't help support a sinful lifestyle, so they lied to us and said they had gotten married. We lived too far away to know one way or the other. The young mother's "granny" down in Texas finally pressured the two of them to truly get married at city hall to get financial help from her as well. She was a tiny spitfire of a woman who adored the Lord with all she was and fiercely loved her family.

We ended up speaking with her as we had gotten a lot of deception from the struggling young couple, and we didn't want to support more immoral behavior. So, we sent money to the little family *through* this lovely, godly granny who made sure it was used for our intended purposes. If they needed furniture, we sent Granny money, and they got furniture. If the baby needed anything, we sent money to Granny, and she made sure they got the car seat, crib, or whatever else the baby needed. We were so thankful God provided us with this wonderful granny, a conduit we could funnel blessings through and know we were no longer duped by these young people who chose to do life the hard way.

Their lifestyle included our son being "responsible" for the baby when his wife went to work, but we don't know how truly responsible he was. We got calls from the "happy couple" while they screamed and fought about his cheating and sinful ways. It was hard to listen to and even harder to fathom a baby and a little girl living amid their dysfunctions.

And then they got pregnant *again.* So frustrated, I wanted to scream, "*Haven't you figured out how this works yet?!*"

But little did we know, our son wasn't just promiscuous; he had developed an alcohol addiction as his morally raised, Bible-literate mind pressed down on his soul and spirit. He knew what was good, true, and right, but he continued to do whatever he wanted instead. So, his conscience would not leave him in peace as he created havoc in so many young lives, not just his own.

He drank heavily.

"… Following the course of this world, following the prince of the power of the air, the spirit that is now at work in the sons of disobedience—among whom we all once lived in the passions of our flesh, carrying out the desires of the body and the mind, and were by nature children of wrath, like the rest of mankind."

(Ephesians 2:2–3)

Things got even more complicated when the next little baby boy came along about a year after his brother (less than two years after his big sister up in Ohio). When it seemed impossible to make things worse, our son pushed the limits on how difficult he could make life and continued to head down into a pit of evil. He continued his descent, where it got darker and darker. You can read further details in the epilogue.

But the odyssey of our prodigal son, Zachariah, gave me a pause to think about how God, as our Father, must feel when we are stubborn and choose our own way. He also sees the heart condition, our motives, behind every choice we make, which could only make it far more crushing than it is for us earthly parents. Especially when His Word makes known to us the right way, the truth.

Sin separates us, from God and each other. We pray, "Thy will be done," but then hesitate, lose our nerve, and turn from His ways because we don't trust His will to be the best thing for us and everyone involved. My life as a parent opened my eyes wide to God's perspective as our heavenly Father. And it has caused me to be far more resolute in seeking His will in my own life.

So, despite the nonsense swirling around us at this juncture, regardless of the dysfunction in which we found ourselves involved, though not embroiled, we had the peace and satisfaction of knowing we were still walking in God's will.

"In His will is our peace."

—Dante

We have the choice to be self-willed or meek and molded by God. Dave and I avoided inner conflict and opted for peace of mind and soul by choosing His way, His will.

So, when people often asked if we were "done" with enlarging our family and being wise after his earlier declaration of no kids after 40, Dave remained quiet. I just said, "I *think* we are done, but God alone knows." And then I had yet another dream.

Amusing Anecdote

We were out to lunch, and one of my young sons had decided he was old enough to order his own meal. When it was his turn, I nodded at him, prompting him to go ahead and order. He asked for his usual, a cheeseburger with no lettuce, tomato, onion or pickles on it and French Fries, his favorite "condiment." Yes, he puts them *on* the cheeseburger.

When the waitress asked him how he would like his burger cooked, he looked at me, and I nodded again to go ahead and tell her. He looked back at the waitress, and with a face as sober as a judge, he said, "Perfectly."

He makes me lie down in green pastures.
He leads me beside still waters. He restores my soul.

(Psalm 23: 2–3a)

11

Dream On and Close It Down

I love it when God does this—letting me have a peek at the cards He's playing. Dreams for me have always been a blessing—the Lord gives me an idea of His will, letting me have an idea of the cards He is playing—what He is doing or where we are headed. But our life was still very much a faith walk; He never promised a spotlight out into the distance—scripture makes it seem more like a little flashlight:

"Your word is a lamp to my feet and a light to my path."

(Psalms 119:105)

My faith in Him trusted He would do what was right and best for all involved, not necessarily what I wanted, was comfortable with, or thought was best. This meant I could trust Him with every next step, one day at a time. If He did call me to put my foot out into complete, utter darkness, He would be faithful to place something firm for me to put my foot down in safety.

"The steps of a man are established by the Lord, when he delights in His way; though he fall, he shall not be cast headlong, for the Lord upholds his hand."

(Psalm 37:23–24)

The next dream from God was simple and lovely without any deep theological meaning. His clarity was bliss. In the dream, I walked in a lush, forested area and came down from a majestic mountainous region—returning from a journey.

In the distance, I saw a tranquil lake with a colonial white-steepled church on a verdant spit of land. Its mirror image was perfectly reflected in the placid lake water. I walked toward it, drawn by the serenity but also because the church is such a wonderful home to me; it's where my Father's family gathers.

As I reached the small peninsula, I looked out toward the mirror-like lake, just beyond the church's reflection and saw a little dot floating on the horizon. It was coming toward me. I walked to the edge of the lake, magnetically pulled, as the dot seemed to be drawn to me in the same way, but I never took my eyes off it.

As I got closer, I saw the dot was in fact, a basket, and the Old Testament story of baby Moses from the book of Exodus immediately popped into my mind's eye. In the scripture, when Moses was born, his mother placed him in a basket made of rushes to save him from being killed by Pharaoh, who had declared an edict that called for the destruction of all Hebrew boys under the age of two. In the second chapter of Exodus, it describes how she sent the basket down the river and watched it carefully until it was rescued by Pharaoh's daughter. Thus, she saved her son Moses from certain death, and he was adopted by the royal family. Such sacrificial mother's love!

What next flashed into my mind was "Oh no, another baby is coming, and Dave is going to be sorely challenged by this." (To be honest, the thought was more like "Oh crap! Dave is going to have a cow!") The basket came slowly to the lake's edge, and with a blend of fear and faith, I knelt down and threw back the cover, and it was … *empty*. Not knowing I'd been holding my breath, I exhaled in relief. Phew!

When I say I had fear and faith, it's because faith isn't believing God would do what I wanted. I can't emphasize enough, I trusted He would do what was right, what was best for all involved. The "terrible twins" had taken a lot out of us, and I just wasn't sure we had more to give. Though if we needed anything, we knew God would provide.

The next morning, Dave listened intently to my recount of the dream and looked somewhat terrified till I got to the very end, the *empty* basket. We were relieved, and from that day forward, we felt comfortable telling anyone who asked about our ever-growing family, we were done having children of our own. It was the end of an era. Our older kids had already started to marry and set up their own households, so our extended family would keep us busy enough.

And busy we have remained as we have submitted to whatever God has called us to. The 37th Psalm states the meek shall inherit the earth and the meek are people willing "to be molded" by God. He couldn't have the self-assured inherit the earth! They'd wreck it! God needs people able to be redirected and recreated in His image. Maturing in our Christian faith over the past decades, Dave and I grew in meekness as we submitted our lives to be molded by God, and it was *such* an adventure.

"For it is God who works in you, both to will and to work for his good pleasure."

(Philippians 2:13)

He didn't call us to be successful—He asked us to be faithful to His calling. He didn't say you would hear "well done my good and *successful* servant," rather, "well done, good and *faithful* servant." (Matthew 25:21, italics my own)

Now, I have some loose ends of this story I want to tie up, so we are going to take a bit of a hike. Literally for me and figuratively for you. Nothing better than strapping on your hiking shoes and drawing those laces together when you have some thinking to do, or you need to bolster a flagging spirit. When the kids were small, I'd take them with me, and they called my mom hikes "forced marches," but the habit was picked up by many of them as a way to sort out life, one trek at a time.

Nathan and his wife, Kristine have gone on a little anniversary getaway, so Dave and I are in Colorado, house-sitting and dog-sitting for them. I love it here. Trailheads are everywhere.

It's late September, still warm, and the aspens are turning their lovely golden autumn-yellow while the sky is the brightest cerulean blue. I have two enthusiastic canine companions: one is a rambunctious German Shorthaired Pointer 10-month-old puppy named Gus, and the other is Ellie, a spirited three-year-old Cockapoo. Thankfully, she is not as wild and crazy as Gus, but Ellie is a nimble little trooper who recently made a huge life transition from Park Avenue office dog in Manhattan to full-time resident in the mountains of Colorado. The three of us are headed out into the mountains to free up Dave to run his Zoom meeting workday at their house without our inadvertent barking or whining interruptions.

I've filled my backpack with water for all three of us and a bit of a snack for the halfway point. My body just doesn't carry enough fuel for the distance on its own anymore. Aging does that. We set off for the trailhead.

Gus and Ellie are raring to go, and we're off. We began by traversing a meadow that stretches on for miles as it skirts the mountain. The rocks crunch under my feet, and with every step, a little puff of dust rises. It's dry, dry, dry.

In other parts of Colorado, hotshot firefighters battle wildfires, and I can smell the scent of campfire, which I usually love. But I know it is wreaking havoc in forests up north, and so it makes my heart heavy. I stop to pray for those fighting the blazes.

The beautiful meadow was a place I'd seen elk graze in the past, and though there are none today, I know it is teeming with other wildlife right below the surface. The beautiful, undulating waves in the long, dry grass remind me of the national anthem and its line "amber waves of grain." The pups and I have trekked through the meadow and made a turn to begin heading up the mountain.

It's a weekday, and only a few people are out and about this afternoon, compared to a typical weekend. I pass a few retirees, but once we achieve higher elevation, the pups and I left most of them behind. The terrain gets more difficult, causing my quads to burn and my lungs to work hard. It's quite like our family life when I thought having eight small children was hard. But the terrain of family life got far more complicated and difficult as the kids grew up, just as this path gets harder as I climb up.

After cresting several thousand feet of vertical change, things open up, I can see more sky, less forest. It's like coming out of a challenging season of life when you've kept your head down and just tried to get through. I was like that for years. Once our ascent reaches above the tree line, the view is breathtakingly beautiful; we can see forever, as if to the curve of the earth. Now the "purple mountains majesty" lyric pops into my head as the gorgeous mountain range before me just appears to go on and on, endlessly. But nothing goes on forever, and I am still pondering life, family, and God.

I pull out our snack, the dogs' water bowl, and my hydro flask. The petite Cockapoo has to drink first because Gus is a wild thing, water and drool just fly! Little Miss Ellie daintily has her fill, and then I let the puppy go to town on the rest. His zeal for every aspect of life is impressive, even just drinking water.

In my contemplative state, I realize Dave and I have been pretty zealous for life ourselves. We never took time to weigh how we would manage when God called us to adopt a child or even just invite someone to live with us for a while. We just forged ahead and trusted Him.

Would we have loved it if we had created a family whose children became believers and went on to have deep and meaningful relationships with God? Of course. They still may. Would we have rejoiced if any one of them had sought to be employed in the workings of the kingdom of God here on earth? Absolutely. They still may.

Our family is like a snapshot of humanity with God: Jesus literally laid down His life, loved us with wide-open arms, and made a good plan for our future success. And how does humanity respond? Just like our kids. Some care, some stand to the side, and others just walk away. But He still loves us no matter what we do, just as Dave and I love all our children, unconditionally. But we have to trust God's timing and whatever plans He has for their lives.

We've planted good seeds in them. But as the Bible tells us, a seed falls to the ground and dies to bring forth life (1 Corinthians 15:36). In

Revelation 2, God said we need to be obedient *unto* death—not until. That means we need to be obedient even if it might *cause* our death. Dave and I laid down our lives for others, and God said it's the greatest kind of love. Hope abides because we sowed valuable seeds of love, responsibility, diligence, respect, righteousness, and the like.

The way plants grow is a wonderful mystery. Only God can take a seed, dirt, and sunshine and make it fruitful.

"Neither he who plants nor he who waters is anything, but only God who gives the growth."

(1 Corinthians 3:7)

Our seedtime as parents is now over. Our period of adoption is done.

But God isn't.

He's just started.

He alone knows the end from the beginning. And how each of our children's lives is going to turn out is between God and each one of His kids—He doesn't have grandchildren. And this is true for everyone, whether they believe it or not.

It's a difficult walk for us as parents of adult children, trying to live life and give meaningful input when they walk a different path than the one we set them on as children. But I did as much myself. I left the Catholic path my parents set me on as a child to answer God's calling on my own life.

He gave all of us free will, which gives latitude for Him to work in an infinite number of ways and on an infinite number of timelines as He has a plan and a purpose for each of us. Sometimes it may seem like you have forever, like these mountains that stretch before me as far as I can see. But I know the range doesn't go on endlessly. I drove here all the way from Ohio across the flat Midwest of America. The mountains *do* end. And though it sometimes feels like we have forever to respond to God, we all just have a certain window of time, which does end.

But He alone can make our life circumstances come to bear on *His* one great objective—He causes us to grow and conform to the loving likeness of His Son as He challenges us to fulfill the purpose for which He created us.

Dave and I sought to obey God and to do what He wanted even when we didn't see results we liked. Despite many obstacles, pain and prejudice, we found our way in the center of His will and therein lies our peace; our eight were just enough to work that truth into our hearts.

It was certainly not through our strengths and abilities we found our calling. But when we reached the end of ourselves, turned to Him in our inadequacy, and meekly surrendered to His purposes, we found satisfaction, fulfillment, and great joy. The real reward is obeying God, then peacefully entrusting Him with the rest. Now Ellie, Gus, and I need to descend from our mountaintop and get on with this great adventure of life.

Peace is joy at rest. Joy is peace dancing.

—*Alistair Begg*

Epilogue

What does life look like after such an atypical childhood? All the kids are off on their own sets of adventures now, and each forges a very different path. Sadly, some paths rarely converge, but others intersect regularly, and we enjoy those loving reunions whenever and wherever they occur.

Our oldest son, Daniel, now lives an active, outdoorsy lifestyle in Denver, Colorado, with his beautiful wife, Amy. Adrenaline courses through their veins regularly in their new homeland, chock full of adventure. They have two successful careers and sweet golden retrievers named Dori and Tula. They love to travel, ski, camp, hike, and do every other wonderful, audacious activity their beautiful state affords. The latest adventure is to become parents of a baby girl soon, and we are sure they will be wonderful.

Our oldest daughter, Sarah, moved back from the East Coast where her first job opportunities were after college. She now lives closer to family in Michigan with her wonderful husband, Peter, and our sweet grandson Deacon. They juggle two successful careers as well as the joys and challenges of parenthood. They love to travel, sail, and entertain. Deacon is a big fan of parks, swings, and bike rides. We thoroughly

The last picture with everyone in it…with the addition of our daughter in law, Amy.

enjoy Peter and Sarah's adult company and get such delight from Deacon's zeal for everything. It's true what they say about grandparenting; it's so much better than being a parent! All the joys with far fewer responsibilities! Peter and Sarah are joyously expecting their second child this year, and Deacon will be an exemplary big brother.

As I mentioned earlier on the hike, like his big brother Dan, our son Nathan also lives in Colorado, with his lovely bride, Kristine. She is our third in-law that grew up in the western Ohio/southern Michigan area. Dave and I theorize the kids are attracted to similar values and priorities found in this region because they all met their spouses elsewhere. Nate and Kristine have those two wonderful hiking companion dogs mentioned earlier, Ellie and Gus, but are also joyously expecting a baby girl in the spring. They, too, love to travel and partake of the wonderful, active lifestyle found in the beautifully rugged mountains of Colorado.

Olive had a baby girl a year ago and is trying to keep custody even though Children's Services has her on their radar as "at risk." She recently called and asked us to take the baby to keep her daughter from being taken into county custody. Unfortunately, my precarious health precluded us from this consideration, plus the clarity of the final adoption dream indicated God's will for us was to no longer be primary parents.

She found her biological family online and went on to mistreat them the way she did us. I was reached by an older biological sister who asked if we had experienced certain behaviors (lying, stealing, manipulating, etc.) when she was growing up, and I regrettably had to confirm her ill-treatment was consistent. We hope and pray she can get things together, if for no other reason than for the well-being of her baby. Sad to say, Olive has been a wandering soul for quite some time and dabbled in every manner of ungodliness, but we do hope the early seeds of love planted by God and her adoptive family will bring forth good fruit in due time. Better sooner than later because she now has a second child on the way.

Zachariah has plateaued a bit but continues to have dalliances with all manner of carnal exploits. It's as though he's a tempest in his own teacup—he whips up ruinous storms of his own destruction. He's no longer with his family, though neither he nor his wife can afford a divorce, and he has been in and out of homeless shelters, jail, and the streets. Zach had a short stint in the army but was discharged for "failure to conform." Sounds like the army had a title for what we had been trying to tell him for years. He needs to give it a spin and try to do things the right way, not just his way.

He has to recognize certain laws by which life works—laws of God you just can't thumb your nose at! You do not see farmers sowing seed in the winter because God has laws about seedtime and harvest; you break them at your own peril. It just *won't work*. God's laws govern the universe, and we need to follow them. Asserting self-rule leads to judgment.

"And this is the judgment: the light has come into the world, and people loved the darkness rather than the light because their works were evil. For everyone who does wicked things hates the light and does not come to the light, lest his works should be exposed."

(John 3:19–20)

A short time ago, he left his rocky, multiyear, Oedipal relationship with a girlfriend in New Jersey. She was five years *my junior*. The veterans' administration in Cleveland is trying to help him stabilize, but he is still his own worst enemy. Our regular warnings during childhood not to "kick against the goads" carried on into adulthood as pleas for rationality.

He finally recognized his need for addiction recovery. The first stop was a detox hospital to get free chemically. Then he went into addiction recovery care for eight to 12 months. We hope and pray he sticks with it, but changing thinking patterns takes a long time.

Dave and I cleaned out his apartment in "the hood" and cleaned up his many debts. My prayer is he will emerge as if from developing fluid, with life coming into accurate focus and in living color. We pray for God's mercy, not justice, on him and his children.

I just recently saw him for the first time in nine years, and he mentioned he had taken childhood and its freedoms from responsibility for granted. Maybe he's waking up to some truth after years of lying to himself and others. With God, there is always hope, but in the meantime, he has a bleeding ulcer, early-stage lung cancer, and has created yet another baby mama, and this one recently gave birth to twins.

Esther had a successful tour with Up with People and then went to college to study theater. She ran into some financial issues halfway through and had to take a break. Dave said she needed some tough love to learn some financial responsibility after we dug her out of several troubles when she was on tour outside the country. She is now an assistant manager at a grocery store chain and is hopefully working her way back to her bliss in theater performance and singing.

She became somewhat radicalized by the Black Lives Matter movement of late and struggles with what she thinks of us and her upbringing in a Caucasian household. We are guilty of being White. She is sadly giving her best friend, Anna, the same cold shoulder. However, since God chose us and called us to parent her, any argument about our skin color should be brought to Him. But Esther's precious life matters so much to us; we brought her home and raised her as our own as we loved and cared for her through thick and thin.

Sadly, she didn't even have the fortitude and conviction for a civilized conversation—unseen hands reached through the phone lines into my chest *via text* and ripped my heart in two. The next day she self-righteously posted on social media someone else's literary piece entitled "Confronting a Racist Mother." We have gotten the silent treatment for over a year now but still love, weep, and pray for her regularly.

We did all we could to give an understanding of Black history to *all* our kids as we took them to museums and underground railroad houses in the North and slave quarters on plantations in the South. We even had them all sit in Rosa Park's seat on the bus at Greenfield Village. (They have the actual bus!) But heritage is not *the* most important thing about a person. Not by a long shot! You had *nothing* to do with it!

Children don't see the world through the lens of racial identity unless they are forced. Our society as a whole is pushing people to primarily see themselves as representatives of a racial category rather than as an individual. It dehumanizes, reduces empathy, and actually causes racism.

We raised our kids to be proud of their accomplishments and character, who they are on the inside, not the outside. No one has anything to do with the color of their skin, hair, or eyes. You can feel appreciative or fortunate or just plain pleased about your heritage, but what you should be most proud of is what you do with it and how you handle it. What are you going to become because of your background?

The higher ideal you *can* be proud of is to be a person who overcomes obstacles. Not that skin color itself is an obstacle, but the history of the world includes repeated efforts to keep down or oppress people of color, and racism takes many shapes. An overcomer can be proud because it's both an accomplishment *and* a character quality.

It's similar to when I see a tall girl who carries herself upright, shoulders back, and confident. I want to give her a high five! I grew up with a six-foot-tall Swedish grandmother, my wonderful Nana Rose. She was a loving, no-nonsense woman who was confident and strong out of necessity, having been widowed early in life. With Nana around, I wasn't *allowed* to even *think* about slouching. Her attentive love and strength put steel in my spine. She planted her thumb at the base of my back and told me to stand up straight! Consequently, I've always carried myself with excellent posture even after arriving at my columnar 5' 11" stature.

Unfortunately, with my height came a multiplicity of challenges, physical, social, and emotional. Dealing with the rejection of boys in high school was painful. Most guys don't reach their full height till after high school because testosterone does its job a bit later in development and over a longer period. They called me "Amazon" to make themselves feel like their lack of height was somehow my fault; "I'm not short, you're just an Amazon!"

I have fielded comments from both shock-faced children and adults, as well, "Wow! You're tall!" as if it weren't obvious to me. But when I was young, it just ground the self-consciousness deeper into my ever-diminishing self-worth. Later, when I got to college and my height wasn't such an issue, my self-esteem had a season of recovery. Despite my respite, I was still half a foot taller than the average woman.

So, I always faced the "too short" clothing challenge. All tall girls do! Why does every department store have a *petite* section and a *plus* section, but no one has a *tall* section?! My ankles and wrists were on display (and cold!) till an online retailer managed to create a line for tall women. I no longer have to try to find pretty colors in the small men's section just to cover my wrists.

I also have large hands and feet, commensurate with my stature. I can palm a basketball if I have a bit of resin on my hand! My shoe size is a healthy double-digit size 11, and though I had the smallest feet in my family growing up, I was often picked on for my long feet outside our home. Everything about me was long: long arms with long hands ending with long fingers and long legs with long feet ending with long toes.

Girls and teens can be catty and cruel, but it continued into adulthood. A close relative had a best friend who referred to me as "Big Foot" for years, lovingly of course. She only said it out loud when she had been drinking, but at a big family wedding, she was in her usual form, making it out to be her "fun" pet name for me. A friend, who was a physician and a man of color, I might add, turned to me and seeing my crestfallen face said, "She gives your gender a bad name." It assuaged my heart a bit because I felt seen. Understood. Even for just that brief moment. And I say all this to point out how my height shaped me as a person, just as skin color can.

When you go awhile without seeing someone like you, you want to shout, "I see you! And I know what you go through!" And *that* is something to be proud of, not your skin, hair, or eyes but being an overcomer who developed the ability to empathize. And *that* is what I want Esther to understand. Allow your unique challenges to make you an overcomer, a stronger, more confident, and compassionate person. We hope and pray the seeds of love planted in our daughter prove to be fruitful in the long run, but only God knows.

Our son Sean chose to be missing from our lives, as well. We don't know what precipitated it because we had no disagreement or event that could have caused his heart to harden against us. Dave thinks he might have made some lifestyle choices he is not proud of and therefore severed his relationship with us. He hates confrontation in all its forms. But just recently he surprised us and showed up for Easter.

I broke down in tears as I hugged him and said, "I miss you!" and all he said was, "I know." *Such* a typical autistic response, void of empathy or understanding. He has been texting us regularly and wants to get together for a barbeque so we can meet his friends. We don't know why he severed relationship nor why he is trying to put it back together. But we'll take it!

Christopher was finally adopted at age four. We were paid by the county to foster him for four years when all we ever wanted was to be Mom and Dad. His birth mom knew how to use the system to her benefit, and the public footed the bills for foster parents, social workers, lawyers, judges, and court costs all in the name of keeping Chris out of a White family. He has graduated high school and is seeking his place in the work world.

Wonderful Michelle still lives with us, no longer the nanny but our dear friend who understands what we go through better than anyone else on the planet. As I tell people curious about our family configuration, "The Bradys wouldn't throw out Alice just because the kids aged out!" We live companionably together after years of "power-parenting" and love to have all the kids home on holidays. Michelle continues to make all their favorite meals and blesses them at every turn. She adopted her own dog, a golden retriever named Conway, and she loves to dote on him to a ridiculous extent. She is gifted by God and loves to be a caretaker, so Conway is a good outlet for her generous nature.

Dave and I both carry worry lines on our faces that seem to spell out names, as expected I suppose. Eight was enough to ensure we never have everyone doing well all at once. Adult kids have adult problems; gone are the days of diaper changing, tying shoes, stepping on sharp toys, and running to practices and appointments. Gone are the days of nagging about orthodontic rubber bands, navigating the seas of teenage hormones, cheering at various games, and the anxiety of teaching new drivers. At times, our life feels like the Good Shepherd who strikes out to find the one stray sheep (Matthew 18:12). They seem to take turns with life's struggles as we fight tooth and nail for each of them, spiritually and otherwise. We do our best to leave our adult kids and grandchildren in God's hands where the most good can be done by prayer.

We send love and anything needed to our grandsons in Texas. They came up to visit once and had a wonderful week of fun with us and got to meet their half-sister in Ohio. Because our granddaughter lives near us, she gets anything she needs, but due to her proximity, we also get to have an ongoing relationship with her. She loves it at our house. Though she has spoken to him on the phone, she has yet to meet her father, Zach, in person. She is already eight years old.

We took her to meet her baby cousin Deacon, and she left the state of Ohio for the first time ever. She got to go on Aunt Sarah and Uncle Peter's boat and saw Canada across the lake from their Michigan home. She was so excited she asked if I would tell her mom she had seen a "whole different country." I said, "You can tell her!" To which she responded, "She'd never believe me!" Dave and I are so very thankful God gave us this child-centric assignment; we love it.

So, to this day, you will find us working within our God-given purpose, loving and caring for children regardless of ability, though now we do it with our grandchildren and at our church every Sunday. Parkside Church has a wonderful special needs ministry that meets the needs of all age levels: Faithful Friends Kids (for little ones with special needs), Faithful Friends Jr. (for older kids and teens) and Faithful Friends (for special needs adults). We play and sing with the kids and teach them from the children's Bible while their parents go to church. Being on duty 24/7 with a special needs child means parents *need* to get to church and recharge their spirits!

We love "our kids" and enjoy every Sunday with them. Most of them are nonverbal, so we look forward to heaven when we will finally know what some of their unintelligible sounds and meaningful looks have meant—we will see Jesus face-to-face, hoping to hear "well done good and faithful servant."

God has never created a child who seeks to live a mediocre, pointless life. He alone can make your life a great adventure, especially after you discover the particular purpose for which He created you! And though you may not always know where it's all going, driving you to distraction and delighting you in equal measure, if you know Him and trust Him, it'll be a thrilling hold-onto-your-hat ride through life as you seek to do His will. Even the hard parts have redemptive value if you remain meek and allow God to lead, teach, and discipline you through it all. And the adventure continues …

ENDNOTE

I have no expectations of understanding, appreciation, or reward here on earth or in heaven. Even God Himself had just one person in 10 return with thanks as seen by the group of lepers He cleansed (Luke 17:11–19). I cannot expect a better return than Jesus, regardless of the purity of my intentions! But time, attention, and love invested in a child is *never* wasted. Obeying God is its own reward; then we must trust Him with the rest.

With God, there is always hope because He is the same yesterday, today and forever (Hebrews 13:8).

I've been told I have quite a large crown waiting for me in heaven—maybe, maybe not. But if I do, I look forward to casting it at Jesus's feet and running off freely into the fields of flowers that never fade or wither. To God be all the glory.

**The purpose of life is not to be happy. It is to be useful,
to be honorable, to be compassionate, to have it make some
difference that you have lived and lived well.**

—*Ralph Waldo Emerson*

LET'S KEEP THE CONVERSATION — GOING! —

 Find out more about our journey and get resources for your own family at **http://trishakcampbell.com.**

 For **special discounts** or bulk purchases, contact Pro Zoe Publishing at **prozoepublishing@gmail.com.**

 Book Trisha Campbell for speaking events by contacting **Pro Zoe Publishing** at **prozoepublishing@gmail.com.**

CONNECT WITH OUR COMMUNITY ON FACEBOOK AT ...

f /Discouragedmoms

f /Trisha-K-Campbell-101405788689538

THANK YOU FOR READING!

If you enjoyed *Eight Was Enough*, please leave a review on Goodreads or on the retailer site where you purchased this book and help me reach more readers like you!

CPSIA information can be obtained
at www.ICGtesting.com
Printed in the USA
BVHW042226151221
624177BV00015B/868

9 781737 484707